Wisdom from Africa

To: Henry Millstein
Thanks for your wonderful
work & editing! May God
bless you always!

Russ Burके

Wisdom from Africa

Theological Reflections on
the Confessions of St. Augustine

RONALD D. BURRIS

Foreword by J. Alfred Smith Sr.

WIPF & STOCK · Eugene, Oregon

WISDOM FROM AFRICA
Theological Reflections on the Confessions of St. Augustine

Wipf & Stock
An Imprint of Wipf and Stock Publishers
199 W. 8th Ave., Suite 3
Eugene, OR 97401

www.wipfandstock.com

PAPERBACK ISBN: 978-1-4982-7948-2
HARDCOVER ISBN: 978-1-4982-7950-5
EBOOK ISBN: 978-1-4982-7949-9

Manufactured in the U.S.A.   10/17/16

This book is dedicated to the memory of my wonderful mother, Imogene L. Burris. I will never forget the endless support you gave to all your children, grandchildren, great-grandchildren, nieces, nephews and strangers, too. You are missed.

Contents

Foreword

SAINT AUGUSTINE, WHOSE LATIN name was Aurelius Augustinius, was born November 13, 354, in Thagaste, now Souk Ahras, Algeria, some forty miles from the North African Coast. He died August 28, 430, in Hippo Regius, now Annaba, Algeria, where he served as bishop of Hippo from 396 to 430 CE.

Augustine wrote many works that have influenced Catholics and Protestants alike, but his *Confessions* remain one of his most popular works. Regarding this work, I am deeply indebted to Professor Ronald Burris for deepening my appreciation of St. Augustine of Hippo, whose prayers have been enriching for my own prayer life. Having identified with St. Augustine's heart hunger for God and his love for the Psalms, there was so much more of him that I needed and desired in understanding him. This need was met when Professor Burris as an intellectual midwife guided me patiently into a close reading of the *Confessions* of Augustine.

Although not an autobiography, the *Confessions* are one of the most complete records of any person's life from the fourth and fifth centuries. Written in Latin between 397 and 400 CE under the original title *Confessions in Thirteen Books*, it was to be read out aloud with each book to be studied as a complete unit. Professor Burris does this for us, with insightful reflections on each topic and important discussion questions at the end of each chapter. This allows for individual reflection or collective dialogue in the academy or local church setting. This beautiful arrangement allows the individual reader or the class instructor to proceed at the comprehension level of the readers. The questions are well crafted and serve as an aid to understanding the written text. Moreover, because Dr. Burris quotes extensively from the *Confessions* in each chapter, a person who has not read the

Confessions will still gain valuable insight by reading *Wisdom from Africa: Theological Reflections on the* Confessions *of St. Augustine.*

Dr. J. Alfred Smith Sr.
Professor Emeritus of Preaching and Church Ministries
American Baptist Seminary of the West
Pastor Emeritus of Allen Temple Baptist Church

Acknowledgments

First, I would like to thank my lovely wife, Lillian Burris, for being a wonderful supporter of my work. I would also like to give a special thanks to Dr. J. Alfred Smith Sr. for his encouragement over the years and for agreeing to write the foreword to this book. Dr. Smith, you have been a wonderful example of what it means to be a pastor/scholar. I would also like to thank my place of employment, the American Baptist Seminary of the West, for allowing me a sabbatical to work on this project. Finally, I want to thank my editor, Dr. Henry Millstein, for agreeing to work on this project.

Introduction

AT THE AMERICAN BAPTIST Seminary of the West, in Berkeley, California, I have the privilege of teaching a course on St. Augustine every other year. Moreover, each time I teach this course I begin with Augustine's *Confessions*. After leading students through the *Confessions* for several years now, I thought it beneficial to offer my own theological reflections to assist students in understanding this great work.

Thus, this book offers an in-depth analysis and theological reflection on the thirteen books of Augustine's *Confessions*. It seeks to cover the major points raised by Augustine in his *Confessions* and discuss them in a way that will give insight and encouragement to the reader. This work does not propose to reflect on every section of every book of the *Confessions* but rather to discuss the major points noted in each book. In addition, thoughtful questions are listed at the end of each chapter, to stimulate further discussion and hopefully encourage personal questions as well.

Because Augustine's *Confessions* are an honest assessment of his failures as well as his final victory in Christ, there is something for everyone in the pages of this work. Consequently, it is my hope that this book will be of value to the scholar, seminary or college student, serious minister, lay Christian or non-Christian alike. Lastly, because I cite Augustine's *Confessions* throughout the book, a person who has not yet read the *Confessions* will still gain valuable insight about the *Confessions* after reading this book.

In chapter 1, we discuss book I of the *Confessions*, in which Augustine begins by praising God and asking a series of questions that are on his heart. Two questions worth noting in this chapter are: What is the origin of the soul? And how can a person contain God? Augustine also praises God throughout book I as he weaves his confessions of sin throughout. He also analyzes the harsh discipline he received as a child, while attending school. He acknowledges his fault here, but criticizes the behaviors of his elders for allowing such harsh treatment. He closes book I with an examination of the negative influence secular literature had upon his life.

In chapter 2, we discuss Augustine's sixteenth year. During this time, Augustine was running wild with his adolescent friends in his hometown of Thagaste. It is during this period that Augustine recalls his theft of pears from a local vineyard. He regrets this sin deeply because he can find no good reason or motive for his behavior. He challenges the reader to consider the influence our friends can have over us and compares his disobedience with an attempt to imitate God. In looking back, Augustine realizes that God was not silent at this period in his life. God was speaking through his mother, but he refused to listen. Augustine concludes book II with the following self-assessment: "Far from your steadfastness I strayed in adolescence, and I became a land of famine."

In chapter 3, we discuss Augustine's nineteenth year and his activities while attending college in Carthage. During this time in his life, Augustine was enjoying the sexual freedom of a young college student away from home. As a student, however, he read Cicero's work *Hortensius* and became a lover of wisdom. In his pursuit of wisdom, he rejected Christianity and became a Manichean. His mother was upset with this but was comforted by a heavenly vision or dream ensuring her that her son would be saved before she departed this life.

In chapter 4, we look on as Augustine was living with an unnamed girl in a relationship similar to marriage. Although not legally married, they had a child together and were faithful to each other as long as they were together. He does not tell us the exact time this relationship began, but it appears it began when he was eighteen or nineteen. Also in book IV, Augustine mentions that at age twenty-one he was inconsolable at the death of a close friend.

In chapter 5, we note that Augustine is careful to point out that he was now twenty-nine years of age. At this time he met the famous Manichaean bishop Faustus. After this meeting he was sorely disappointed. He did not immediately sever ties with the group, but his respect for them was severely damaged at finding that Faustus was not able to answer his questions in a way that was convincing. Augustine was able to see God's providence in this. For the great Faustus, who ensnared many, actually was used by God to free him. This freedom, however, was also brought about by the preaching of Bishop Ambrose.

In chapter 6, we read of Augustine announcing to his mother that he was no longer a Manichaean, but not yet a Christian. At this, she was overjoyed and prayed even harder for his salvation. Augustine was now listening to the preaching of the great Ambrose and was beginning to appreciate Christian Scripture. Augustine describes his encounter at this time (his thirtieth year) with a beggar on his way to a speaking engagement. Upon seeing the drunken beggar, Augustine was forced to examine his own life and that of his friends. He did so and was sorely disappointed. Augustine concludes book VI with the devastating effects he suffered at his separation from his common-law wife.

In chapter 7, we follow Augustine as he takes a break from an autobiographical sketch of his life to discuss in detail a few theological issues that are on his heart. The two most pressing are his thoughts about God and the problem of evil. Augustine also discusses his final break with astrology. He then closes book VII with an account of one of his several visions that he has noted in this chapter.

In chapter 8, we read of Augustine discussing in detail his final struggles on his way to being converted to Christianity. The tensions that have been building from books I through VII are finally resolved at the end of book VIII. One by one, Augustine's props were knocked out from under him. He received sound advice from Simplicianus on how Victorinus (someone like himself) was saved. He also received instructions from a fellow African, Ponticianus, who spoke to him about the gospel and the great St. Antony. All of this brought him to the point of tears and ultimately to salvation.

Chapter 9 tells of the beginning of Augustine's journey with God. He was baptized in Milan with his son and a few of his friends. His mother was overjoyed that her son had finally become a Christian. However, there was much sadness as Augustine is surrounded by death. Two of his friends, Verecundus and Nebridius, die. Shortly after that, Monnica dies, and then his son Adeodatus dies. He finds comfort in the psalms of David.

In chapter 10, Augustine begins by examining the benefit others might receive from reading his *Confessions*. He then discusses, in much detail, the use of his mind/memory in understanding the inward part of himself and how this inward part can help us know God in a deeper way. Augustine comes to realize that it is with our mind that we come to know and love God.

Chapter 11 discusses book XI, which Augustine begins with a prayer petitioning God for understanding. He then proceeds with a discussion on how God made heaven and earth. God created by his Word, yet the Eternal Word is different from the words we speak in time. Augustine thus distinguishes between human time and God's eternity and moves on to a discussion of human time, challenging us to rethink our understanding of past, present, and future time. He concludes book XI with a consideration of how the human mind can better understand the mystery of time.

Chapter 12 considers Augustine's continuing discussion of creation in book XII, where the saint focuses on how formless matter was used in the process. Augustine also asserts that he is open to various interpretations of the creation narrative (Genesis 1:1–2) as long as they hold some truth in them. Toward the end of book XII (section 19.28) he outlines nine points he believes are true regarding creation.

Chapter 13 moves to the final book of the *Confessions*, book XIII, in which Augustine explores various hidden or allegorical meaning that he believes can be extracted from the scriptural account of creation. He then proceeds to discuss the Trinity, with an emphasis on the Holy Spirit and the possible reasons why Scripture described the Holy Spirit as "hovering over the waters" in the Genesis account. Augustine then challenges his readers to examine the Trinity within themselves. As he pursues the meanings he believes to be hidden in Scripture, he concludes the *Confessions* with a final plea for God's wisdom: "Let us rather ask of you, seek in you, knock at your door. Only so we will receive, only so find, and only so will the door be opened to us. Amen."

1

Infancy and Boyhood

AUGUSTINE BEGINS BOOK I of his *Confessions* by praising God and at the same time confessing what he has come to know about God: that lost souls are still a part of God's creation. Moreover, lost souls desire to praise God, even though they may fail to realize this because they are racked with sin and pride. Augustine insists that such lost souls are restless until they find rest in God. But he also realizes that God is the one drawing lost and restless souls to himself. So he states in his opening:

> Great are you, O Lord, and exceedingly worthy of praise, your power is immense, and your wisdom beyond reckoning. And so we humans, who are a part of your creation, long to praise you— we who carry our mortality about with us, carry the evidence of our sin and with it the proof that you thwart the proud. Yet these humans, due part of your creation as they are, still do long to praise you. You stir us so that praising you may bring us joy, because you have made us and drawn us to yourself, and our heart is unquiet until it rest in you.[1]

After his opening statement of praise, Augustine begins to ask God a series of interrelated questions: "Grant me to know and understand, Lord, which comes first: to call upon you or to praise you? To know you or to call upon you? Must we know you before we can call upon you?" (*Conf.* I.1.1). After presenting these questions, it is as if Augustine pauses and asks how

---

1. Augustine, *Confessions*, I.1.1. All quotations from the *Confessions* are taken from the translation by Maria Boulding, OSB.

a person can call upon a God that is unknown to him; he might make a mistake and call upon the wrong deity. And if that is possible, must we not first know the Lord so we can be certain from whom we are invoking a response? But how can anyone know and believe in God without a preacher? Surely on this point, Augustine is reflecting upon his past life and how he followed the wrong path for so long, thinking it was the right path—something every Christian can relate to. But he continues to puzzle over how he came finally to believe and call upon the Lord. What came first: his seeking or the Lord's drawing? In a sense, the whole of the *Confessions* (and much else in Augustine's work) is an extended wrestling with this question. Here, at the head of his *Confessions*, he provides at least a tentative answer that is true to his experience, as he confesses to his readers the truth of what he has discovered: "But scripture[2] tells us that those who seek the Lord will praise him, for as they seek they find him, and on finding him they praise him" (*Conf.* I.1.1). This Scripture was fulfilled in Augustine's life, for he sought the Lord and found him. Now he is forever ready to praise God whom he has come to know. Though Augustine cannot tell for certain what came first in our final acceptance of salvation, he declares to the Lord something we should all consider: "Let me seek you then, Lord, even while I am calling upon you, and call upon you even as I believe in you, for to us you have indeed been preached" (*Conf.* I.1.1). In Augustine's case, it was the gifted preaching of Bishop Ambrose of Milan that brought him to the truth of God's salvation. But now that he is saved, he will continue to seek and call upon the Lord as he confesses his sins and praises God for the gift of salvation. Thus his *Confessions* take on the form of a prayer: sometimes a prayer of praise and worship, and other times the prayer of a sinner questioning his maker about deep truths he has yet to learn.

In sections 1.2 to 4.4 of book I, Augustine asks another series of questions to which he does not appear to have the answers; in asking these questions, he hopes to receive some enlightenment to help his limited understanding. Before Augustine was saved, he believed that the Catholic Church taught that God had a physical body. This bothered Augustine greatly, because any deity with a physical body would have limitations, and God, to be God, must be without limitations. However, after listening to the preaching of Bishop Ambrose, he realized that the Catholic Church did not hold this view, thus removing an obstacle on the path to salvation for him. Consequently, by the time of his *Confessions*, he believed that God was

2. Rom 10:14.

a spiritual being that dwells in each believer; but that belief raises further questions: "How shall I call upon my God, my God and my Lord, when by the very act of calling upon him I would be calling him into myself ?[3] Is there any place within me into which my God might come?" (*Conf.* I.2.2). And before he attempts to answer these questions, Augustine asks yet more questions to let us know what he is getting at: how can God, whom heaven and earth cannot contain, dwell within a frail human body? And how can a human being call God into himself, when a human being cannot even exist unless God is within him or her? Augustine reasons: "Since nothing that exists would exist without you, does it follow that whatever exists does in some way contain you?" (*Conf.* I.2.2).

Augustine expresses these mounting dilemmas as follows:

> Should we suppose, then, that because all things are incapable of containing the whole of you, they hold only a part of you, and all of them the same part? Or does each thing hold a different part, greater things larger parts, and lesser things smaller parts? Does it even make sense to speak of larger and smaller parts of you? Are you not everywhere in your whole being, while there is nothing whatever that can hold you entirely?[4]

Augustine is certain that God dwells in him and in his creation, even if he cannot tell us how this is possible. He knows this indwelling of God to be a reality, and this causes him to praise God and speak of what he does know about God from Scripture and experience. The mysteries expressed here lead Augustine to conclude with a cascade of paradoxes:

> What are you, then my God? What are you, I ask, but the Lord God? For who else is lord except the Lord, or who is god if not our God? You are most high, excellent, most powerful, omnipotent, supremely merciful and supremely just, most hidden yet intimately present, infinitely beautiful and infinitely strong, steadfast yet elusive, unchanging yourself though you control the change in all things, never new, never old, renewing all things yet wearing down the proud though they know it not; ever active, ever at rest, gathering while knowing no need, supporting and filling and guarding, creating and nurturing and perfecting, seeking although you lack nothing. You love without frenzy, you are jealous yet secure, you regret without sadness, you grow angry yet remain tranquil, you

---

3. "To invoke (Latin *invocare*) is to call in: How can Augustine 'call in' God who made heaven and earth?" Clark, *Augustine*, 35.

4. *Confessions*, I.3.3.

alter your works but never your plan; you take back what you find although you never lost it; you are never in need yet you rejoice in your gains, never avaricious yet you demand profits. You allow us to pay you more than you demand, and so you become our debtor, yet which of us possesses anything that does not already belong to you? You owe us nothing, yet you pay your debts; you write off our debts to you, yet you lose nothing thereby.[5]

After Augustine has described God as best he can, he refers to God as "my God, my life, my holy sweetness" (*Conf.* I.4.4). Yet with all of these wonderful adjectives he uses in describing God, he realizes that these words are still inadequate for the task at hand. Nonetheless, he also realizes that those who love God must speak, even if they fall short. For not to speak is worse.

Augustine's attention has been focused on the mystery of God; now he begins to look inward. In section 5.5, Augustine asks that God grant him peace and enable him to forget the evil that he is facing. In the opening of the *Confessions*, Augustine has already declared that God has given him peace and rest, yet he is not contradicting himself here. No, what Augustine seeks here is a deeper relationship with God. So he declares, "O Lord my God, tell me what you are to me. Say to my soul, *I am your salvation.*[6] Say it so that I can hear it. My heart is listening" (*Conf.* I.5.5). Augustine wants more of God, so he speaks in such a way that God will hear him. And every believer would do well to follow him on this point. He lays his heart bare and speaks the truth about his failings. Augustine declares that the "house of his soul is too small for God to enter" so he pleads with God to make it more spacious (*Conf.* I.5.6). Indeed, he confesses not only that his soul is too small but also that it lies in ruins, so he pleads with God to forgive him, as he knows God will see things that will be offensive. Having laid his sins bare before God, he is certain that God has forgiven the wickedness of his heart. So he concludes, "I do not argue my case against you, for you are truth itself; nor do I wish to deceive myself, lest my iniquity be caught in its own lies. No, I do not argue the case with you, because *if you Lord keep the score of our iniquities, then who, Lord, can bear it?*" (*Conf.* I.5.6).[7] One of Augustine's favorite names for God is "Truth." Because God is "truth itself" one must not argue with God as if to defend oneself. On the contrary, one

---

5. Ibid., I.4.4.

6. Ps 34:3 (35:3).

7. Ps 129:3 (131:3).

must confess one's sins while seeking mercy from an all-knowing God. This revelation is liberating for Augustine, for he now realizes that he can ask God anything, if he speaks the truth from his heart—for God, who is truth, will not reject his truthful inquiries. This, I believe, is the basis for Augustine's freedom in questioning God throughout his *Confessions*: he knows God can handle his sincere invocations. This leads us to our next section.

Augustine is now ready to ask one of his more challenging questions. Perhaps he is aware that this question is unusual, for he prepares it with the following plea: "Yet allow me to speak, though I am but dust and ashes, allow me to speak in your merciful presence, for it is to your mercy that I address myself, not to some man who would mock me." He then feels free to ask, "What is it that I am trying to say, Lord, except that I do not know whence I came into this life that is but a dying, or rather, this dying state that lead to life?" (*Conf.* I.6.7). A little further in his *Confessions*, Augustine will ask this question again, but with more specificity. Here he continues:

> Tell me, I beg you, tell your miserable suppliant, O merciful God, whether my infancy was itself the sequel to some earlier age, now dead and gone. Was there nothing before it, except the life I lived in my mother's womb? Some information about that has been given me, and I have myself seen pregnant women. But then, my God, my sweetness, what came before that? Was I somewhere else? Was I even someone? I have nobody to tell me: neither father nor mother could enlighten me, nor the experience of others, nor any memory of my own. Are you laughing at me for asking you these questions, and are you perhaps commanding me to praise you and confess to you simply about what I do know?[8]

Augustine here raises the question of the origin of the soul. His contemporaries proposed three theories concerning the origin of the soul. The Traducian or Generation theory taught that the soul originates from the body of our parents at conception. The Creationist theory taught that each individual soul is a direct creative act by God; God was seen as continually creating souls every time a child is born. And, third, the Preexistence theory taught that our soul existed prior to birth. At this time in Augustine's career, we know that Augustine disapproved of the Creationist theory. In his exegesis of Genesis 1 in the *Confessions* (XI.7–9; XII.5.18), Augustine rejects the Creationist view by maintaining that God created the world through his Word (that is Jesus) out of nothing, and that this creative act was not done

8. *Confessions*, I.8.9.

piecemeal; that is, God did not speak and create one thing and then speak again and create another thing. On the contrary, Augustine insisted that God gave one utterance, causing all things to be created simultaneously in one eternal speaking. Were this not so, he argued, time and change would come into eternity, and thus there would be no true eternity.

For years, Augustine also had problems with the Traducian view, but in later years in his debate with the Pelagians, he leaned toward this view, because it best supported his doctrine of original sin. The Traducian view easily supported Augustine's conviction that every human is connected to the sin of our first parents in the garden of Eden. At the time he wrote the *Confessions*, however, Augustine rejected the Creationist view and viewed the Traducian theory with some hesitation. The only theory left was that of the preexistence of souls, but Augustine was not certain he could endorse that view either, leaving him with no clear answer to the question. So we can certainly understand why Augustine raised questions about the Preexistence view with such passion. In this passage he begs God to tell him, what, if his birth was a sequel to something, which preceded it. And he goes on to ask: "Was I somewhere else? Was I even someone?" (*Conf.* I.6.9).

All three theories have theological implications, and I believe that Augustine is begging God for insight into this most difficult question because it can give an orientation to one's theological thinking on several issues. For example, a perfect soul joined to the human body at conception has very different theological implications (in particular, for one's view of salvation) from a tainted soul joined to the human body. Augustine, like other church fathers, wanted to argue that infants, having inherited the sin of Adam and Eve, needed baptism because of their fallen state; the Traducianist view was most compatible with this assertion.[9] It is no surprise, therefore, that Augustine ultimately rejected the Preexistence view about which he raises such passionate questions here.[10]

Having considered the origin of the soul, Augustine moves naturally in section 6.10 to questions about humanity's dependence on God and from there to a consideration of the nature of God's eternity. He asks in various ways how any person could exist apart from God. He reasons that certainly we could not have made ourselves and equally certainly we could not exist apart from God. Yet God is different from us in that our days pass

9. For a discussion on baptism in North Africa, see Burris, *Where Is the Church*, ch. 3.

10. For a discussion of the preexistence of the soul and memory, see O'Connell, *St. Augustine's Confessions*, 42–43.

away but God's days do not pass away. In view of this reality, he strives to understand God's relationship to time. In Augustine's view, time exists for God as one eternal, present "Today." He states, "yet you are the selfsame: all our tomorrows and beyond, all our yesterdays and further back, you will make in your Today, you have made in your Today." Augustine anticipates the difficulty his readers may have (perhaps echoing the difficulty he himself has) in following this, so he declares. "What does it matter to me, if someone does not understand this? Let such a person rejoice even to ask the question. 'What does this mean?' Yes, let him rejoice in that, and choose to find by not finding rather than by finding fail to find you" (*Conf.* I.7.10). This statement is very telling, and something of which we may need to remind ourselves from time to time as we discuss his *Confessions*. Augustine knows how far he has come; he recognizes the errors that he had previously embraced. Now he is happy to ask questions, he must ask questions, for they are on his heart, and he is still a seeker of wisdom.[11] And if someone wants to criticize him, he can accept that criticism, but he will continue to insist that the most important thing is to know God, even if a person fails to find all the answers. In fact, we should rejoice that we have a mind to ask.

In section 7.11, Augustine returns to the issue of sin. He is well aware of his past sinful life and at times seems almost obsessed with the issue of sin. Certainly, in his *Confessions*, he will not only confess his sins to God but also make every effort to understand and explain the very nature of sin and its origin. Thus he begins section 7.11 with the following statement:

> Alas for the sins of humankind! A human it is who here bewails them and you treat him mercifully because you made him, though the sin that is in him is not of your making. Who is there to remind me of the sin of my infancy (for sins there was: no one is free from sin in your sight, not even an infant whose span of earthly life is but a single day); who can remind me of it?[12]

Notice that Augustine refers above to the "sins of humankind." Because of the sin of Adam and Eve in the garden of Eden, Augustine must refer to sin as belonging to "humankind." He is careful to separate the sin of humankind from God. For Augustine, God is not the author of our sin. Our sin is connected to our corrupt nature inherited by our first parents and to our will, as he will discuss later. As a result of this belief, however, Augustine

---

11. Augustine fell in love with wisdom after reading Cicero's *Hortensius* (III.4.7–8). This happened before he was saved, but now that he is saved, he is still a seeker of wisdom.

12. *Confessions*, I.7.11.

insists that babies, even one day old, are not free from sin. He then cites some of the sins he believes babies are guilty of committing. Of course, he does not remember his own sins at this age, but from his observation of other infants, Augustine declares, "The only innocent feature in babies is the weakness of their frame" (*Conf.* I.7.11). He has personally seen the fury of infants toward other babies; he has seen them throwing tantrums. To reinforce his belief on this point, he cites a verse from Psalm 51:5. This is a famous psalm attributed to King David as the words he spoke after his sinful relationship with Bathsheba. Again, Augustine puts this verse in the form of a question: "And if I was even conceived in iniquity, and with sin my mother nourished me in her womb, where, I beg of you, my God, where was I, your servant, ever innocent: Where, Lord and when?" (*Conf.* I.7.12). The answer inferred from this verse and from verses in the New Testament (e.g., Rom 5:8) is that humankind is not innocent and has never been innocent.[13] We came into this world with a tainted nature and therefore we are not innocent. Even after baptism, Augustine insists, we are not completely healed from our fallen nature.[14]

In the next sections (*Conf.* I.9.14f.) Augustine moves on to events in his early childhood that he can recall with much detail. It is unquestionably true that certain events in our life, particularly traumatic events, will stand out in our minds for years. And so it was with Augustine's experience at school. He recalls:

> Ah, God, my, God, what wretchedness I suffered in that world, and how I was trifled with! The program for right living presented to me as a boy was that I must obey my mentors, so that I might get on in this world and excel in the skills of the tongue, skills which lead to high repute and deceitful riches. To this end I was sent to school to learn my letters, though I, poor wretch, could see no point in them. All the same, I would be beaten whenever I was lazy about learning. This punishment was taken for granted by grown-up people and many a pupil had undergone it before we did, laying down those rough roadways along which we were

13 According to the doctrine of original sin as taught by Augustine and other Western church leaders, babies come into the world tainted by the sin of our first parents, Adam and Eve. See Augustine's work *On Nature and Grace* for a discussion of his views on original sin.

14 Julian of Eclanum (ca. 386–ca. 455), challenged Augustine, saying that if baptism cleanses us from sin, then the children of baptized parents should be free from the taint of original sin. In response to this, Augustine taught that even baptized persons are not totally clean from the effects of original sin.

now being driven, as we bore our part in the heavy labor and pain allotted to the sons of Adam.[15]

In recalling his instruction at school, Augustine is very critical of the beatings inflicted on him by his instructors for not working up to his full potential. He even compares his childhood beatings with the harsh treatment adults received while being tortured under rack and hook. He points out that no one would dare make light of such treatment of adults, but this is what happened to the children. His parents and other elders not only approved of this harsh discipline but even laughed about it when it was brought to their attention. Augustine looks back on this period in his life with a certain horror and recalls how he prayed earnestly to God for the beating to stop, but God did not hear his plea. He reasons that God refrained "lest by hearing it you might have consigned me to a fool's fate" (*Conf.* I.9.14). Augustine will not accuse God, for he believes that God allowed this to happen to him for his future benefit, but he can accuse others, and accuse he does. After admitting that he was guilty of not working up to his potential because of his love of playing games, Augustine blames his instructors for the same fault. He charges that the adults in his community were also guilty of playing games, but they called their games "business." Here, Augustine is referring to the public entertainments that were provided by well-to-do citizens and attended by the residents of the town. The irony, however, is that the citizens who provided these shows wanted their children (who received beatings for playing games at school) to receive a good education so they could provide these shows—or games—when they became adults. In Augustine's recollection of his mistreatment at school, he is offering the reader an opportunity to ponder his or her core values and sense of fairness. For example, what are we really preparing our children to become in life? Are we preparing them for a career only to make money that has little value in the eyes of God? Or, as Augustine might ask, preparing them to play an even uglier game than the ones we are now playing ourselves? And if we can condemn their behavior, can we adults also examine our own?

Augustine recalls becoming gravely ill during this period and begging his mother to have him baptized. She considered it, but because of his rapid recovery from his illness, she decided against baptizing him at that time. Augustine speaks to this, saying: "My cleansing was therefore deferred on the pretext that if I lived I would inevitably soil myself again, for it was

15. *Confessions*, I.9.14.

9

held that the guilt of sinful defilement incurred after the laver of baptism was graver and more perilous" (*Conf.* I.11.17).[16] During this time, many Christians put off baptism until they were married and ready to live a life more dedicated to the Lord. Augustine challenges this practice, pointing out that we do not put off sending our loved ones to the doctor if they have a sickness in their body; how much more, then, should every effort be made to have our soul be in good health and right standing with God? Of course, the very sins from which his mother sought to shield him by deferring his baptism were the sins he found himself committing after his recovery. Nonetheless, Augustine sees the hand of God at work here, in spite of the various contradictions. He insists:

> But you, who have even kept count of our hairs, turned to my profit the misguided views of those who stood over me and made me learn, just as you also turned to my profit my own perverse unwillingness to learn by using it to punish me, for I certainly deserved punishment, being a great sinner for such a tiny boy. In this way you turned to my good the actions of those who were doing no good, and gave me my just deserts by means of my sin itself. Matters are so arranged at your command that every disordered soul is its own punishment.[17]

As Augustine closes book I, he evaluates the literature he was taught as a child and the effect it had on him. For instance, he recalls how he would weep over Dido, who killed herself for love, but never wept over himself, who was spiritually dead. Of course he did not understand his desperate spiritual state at the time, but now his past sins cause him much grief. Augustine also takes to task the writings of Homer and suggests that they had a part to play in his wickedness:

> Who among our hooded masters of oratory gave sober thought to the cry of one who was of the same clay as themselves, "Homer invented these stories and attributed human actions to the gods, but I wish he had rather provided us with examples of divine behavior"? It would be truer to say that Homer did indeed make up

16. In the early church, many put off baptism because of the problem of committing post-baptismal sins. Because baptism was the point in which one entered the church and a sacrament that was not to be repeated, new converts were naturally very cautious before they got baptized. The unintended consequence, however, was that many persons put off baptism for years, some until the end of their life. Augustine was critical of this practice.

17. *Confessions*, I.12.19.

these tales, and thereby seemed to invest the disgraceful deeds of human beings with an aura of divinity, so that depraved actions should be reckoned depraved no longer, since anyone who behaved so could pretend to be imitating not abandoned humans but the gods above.[18]

And he has this to say of Terence:

> Could we not have learned those useful words elsewhere, words like "shower," "golden," "lap," "trick," "heavenly temples," if Terence had not presented to us a young scoundrel who took Jupiter as a model for his own fornication? This young man looks at a mural painting which shows how Jupiter tricked a woman by sending a golden shower in Danae's lap. Watch the dissolute youth making use of heavenly instruction to work up his lust! "What a god!" he exclaims, "a god who makes the temples of heaven ring with his thunder!" Well, a poor little fellow like me can't do that, but I have imitated him in the other thing, and what fun it was![19]

The last line is telling: "I have imitated him in the other thing, and what fun it was." Perhaps Augustine is ahead of his time in pointing out the influence literature can have on an individual.

When assessing his education, Augustine at times sounds like the Apostle Paul in his letter to the Philippians. In Philippians 3:8, Paul says his old life under the law was like horse manure in comparison to knowing Christ. Augustine seems to be making the same point; now that he has come to appreciate Scripture, he is very critical of what he learned in the world and how he learned it. Some of this in expressed in one of his many prayers:

> Hear my prayer, Lord. Let not my soul faint under your discipline, nor let me weary as I confess before you those acts of mercy by which you plucked me from all my evil ways. I long for you to grow sweeter to me than all those allurements I was pursuing. You have enabled me to love you with all my strength and with passionate yearning grasp your hand, so that you may rescue me from every temptation until my life's end.[20]

Augustine concludes book one with a fitting praise, which acts as a pause before he begins again to utter the rest of his *Confessions*:

18. Ibid., I.16.25.
19. Ibid., I.16.26.
20. Ibid., I.15.24.

In a living creature such as this
everything is wonderful and worthy of praise,
but all these things are gifts from my God.
I did not endow myself with them,
but they are good, and together they make me what I am.
He who made me is good, and he is my good too;
rejoicing, I thank him for all those good gifts
which made me what I was, even as a boy.
In this lay my sin,
that not in him was I seeking pleasures, distinctions and truth,
but in myself and the rest of his creatures,
and so I fell headlong into pains, confusions and errors.
But I give thanks to you, my sweetness, my honor, my confidence;
to you, my God, I give thanks for your gifts.
Do you preserve them for me.
So will you preserve me too,
and what you have given me will grow and reach perfection,
and I will be with you; because this too is your gift to me
—that I exist.[21]

21. Ibid., I.20.31.

DISCUSSION QUESTIONS FOR CHAPTER 1

1. Discuss Augustine's opening praise in section 1.1 and one or more of his questions that he poses to God.

2. What would you call Augustine's *Confessions* up to this point: prayer, praise, confession, or worship?

3. Why do you think Augustine asks so many questions of God? Can you relate to this approach?

4. Why did Augustine have a problem with God having a physical body?

5. In section 4.4 Augustine describes God as best he can. Is there any word or phrase that stands out in your mind?

6. Why do you think Augustine said, "Those who love God must speak"? And what does he mean by this?

7. Why did Augustine say, "I do not argue my case with you, because *if you keep the score of our iniquities, then who, Lord, can bear it?*"

8. Do you agree or disagree that it is liberating for Augustine to ask God all the questions that are on his heart? Can we learn anything from this?

9. Discuss the three theories regarding the origin of the soul? Do you prefer any one theory to the other two? Do you have any views about the origin of the soul not mentioned here?

10. What does Augustine mean by the "sins of humankind"?

11. Discuss Augustine's reaction to being beaten at school and his assessment of this punishment.

12. Why did Augustine's mother refuse him baptism when he became sick at an early age? Was this the right thing to do? Do we behave like this today?

13. What does Augustine have to say about the literature he read and how it influenced him?

14. Is Augustine ahead of his time in speaking about this influence or is this an excuse for his behavior?

15. What issue/s did Augustine discuss in book one that is/are relevant for our consideration today?

2

Adolescence

In book II of his *Confessions*, Augustine informs us that during his sixteenth year he had a break in his education that caused him to return to his hometown of Thagaste, because his father was saving money for him to attend a better school in Carthage. Augustine spent this enforced vacation wandering the streets of Thagaste with his rowdy friends. In recalling this period of his life, Augustine is careful to mention the sad and sinful life he lived as a young adolescent. He does not hold back in describing his morally depraved condition. He informs the reader, however, that he is not confessing his sins because he loves them; rather he hopes that by confessing them he will love God more and so find God's presence in his life even sweeter:

> Now I want to call to mind the foul deeds I committed, those of the flesh that corrupted my soul, not in order to love them, but to love you, my God. Out of love for loving you I do this, recalling my most wicked ways and thinking over the past with bitterness so that you may grow ever sweeter to me; for you are a sweetness that deceives not, a sweetness blissful and serene. I will try now to give a coherent account of my disintegrated self, for when I turned away from you, the one God, and pursued a multitude of things, I went to pieces. There was a time in adolescence when I was afire to take my fill of hell. I boldly thrust out rank, luxuriant growth in various furtive love affairs; my beauty wasted away and I rotted

in your sight, intent on pleasing myself and winning favor in the eyes of men.[1]

In accord with this statement, Augustine throughout book II offers the reader—whether senior pastor, youth minister, or anyone else interested—a way to have an honest discussion about the pitfalls teenagers face when sexually active. For example, Augustine admits that being sexually active at such a young age made him lose control of his desires. Moreover, he confesses that he could not even distinguish between lust and love, stating that "the two swirled about together and dragged me, young and weak as I was, over the cliffs of my desires, and engulfed me in a whirlpool of sins" (*Conf.* II.2.2). As Augustine looks back on this period in his life, he realizes that being sexually active and idle at such a young age brought on moral disaster. It caused him to live a life that he is ashamed to discuss, except in confessing his sins to God that he may hate those sins and love God more.

He wonders if things would have come out differently had his parents arranged a marriage for him. His mother did in fact warn him not to fornicate and to avoid at all cost sexual relations with another man's wife. But because of his academic potential she did not arrange a marriage for him, thinking it might hinder his opportunity to succeed. Augustine does seem to find this decision unfortunate, for he complains that "none of my family made any attempt to avert my ruin by arranging a marriage for me," thus leaving him prey to "a lust that [was] licensed by disgraceful human custom, but illicit before your [i.e., God's] laws" (*Conf.* II.4.4). Augustine may well have been right in supposing that marriage might have brought him some mastery over his desires, for when he did get a live-in lover a year or so later, he did not continue his sexual exploits. The two had a child together, lived in a state of marriage (though not legally married), and were faithful to each other as long as they were together.[2] All this brings Augustine to wonder if God was silent during this period in his life. He asks: "Do I dare to say that you were silent, my God, when I was straying from you?" Yet, after asking this question, Augustine seems to recoil, and he challenges himself: "Were you really silent to me at that time"? (*Conf.* II.3.7). The implied answer is clearly in the negative. He realizes that God was speaking to him through his mother, Monnica, but he was not ready to listen: when he scorned his mother's advice, he was in fact scorning God. For God was

---

1. *Confessions*, II.1.1.

2. In many ways it was like a marriage and could be called a marriage, except in name.

indeed speaking to him through her, but he refused to hear. But how could he hear, when his pride and need to be admired by his friends caused him to compete to be the most sinful among his companions? Augustine recalls in detail his sad condition:

> But I was quite reckless; I rushed on headlong in such blindness that when I heard other youths of my own age bragging about their immoralities I was ashamed to be less depraved than they. The more disgraceful their deeds, the more credit they claimed; and so I too became as lustful for the plaudits as for the lechery itself. What is more to be reviled than vile debauchery? Afraid of being reviled I grew viler, and when I had no indecent acts to admit that could put me on a level with these abandoned youths, I pretended to obscenities I had not committed, lest I might be thought less courageous for being more innocent, and be accounted cheaper for being more chaste.[3]

Augustine offers here an honest assessment of what often happens among groups of young people. Their need to be accepted among the group becomes greater than their need to maintain their moral bearings. As a result, they will often follow the group without thinking through their actions. This certainly is what happened to Augustine, as he re-examines his sixteenth year from a new perspective. Not only did he confess to sins he did not commit, but one night he and his comrades stole pears from a nearby vineyard. This bothers Augustine greatly, because he did not steal the pears out of need, for he had better fruit at home. Nor did he steal the pears because he wanted to eat them; they did not even taste good—as noted, he had tastier ones at home. He can find no good reason for his theft, and this causes him to break out in prayer to God before he continues:

> Look upon my heart, O God, look upon this heart of mine, on which you took pity in its abysmal depths. Enable my heart to tell you now what it was seeking in this action which made me bad for no reason, in which there was no motive for my malice except malice. The malice was loathsome, and I loved it. I was in love with my own ruin, in love with decay: not with the thing for which I was falling into decay but with decay itself, for I was depraved in soul, and I leapt down from your strong support into destruction, hungering not for some advantage to be gained by the foul deed, but for the foulness of it.[4]

3. *Confessions*, II.3.7.
4. Ibid., II.4.9.

Augustine spends eight sections of book II discussing his theft of the pears. To him, this is not some childhood prank that can be laughed at and forgotten. No, this sin has far deeper significance for him. Augustine is troubled by his inability to discern a sensible motive for his actions.[5] In the passage just quoted, he states that his motive for stealing the pears was malice. In other passages, he writes that he did it for the love of the theft. So Augustine has given motives for his theft, but these motives do not satisfy him, so he must go deeper.

In his attempt to do so, Augustine discusses the question of the nature of what is good in life. He informs us that there are many material things that attract our eyes and are—at least in certain ways—good. Things like gold, silver, and other precious metals are good. There is also a good that can be found in other, nonmaterial aspects of life. For example, Augustine notes that even our bonds with other people can be a good: "The friendship which draws humans being together in a tender bond is sweet to us because out of many minds it forges a unity" (*Conf.* II.5.10). So material things such as gold and silver can be a good, friendship can be a good, and the pears which he stole are in themselves good, because God created them. Yet Augustine insists that these lower goods can lead a person to sin when they are used improperly, that is, when we focus on lower goods to the detriment of the higher good. Of course, the higher good which brings us true happiness and joy is God, God's truth, and God's law. Why then, Augustine asks himself, did he seek the lower good at the expense of the higher? What was his motive? Augustine reasons that even a murderer will have a motive for his actions. Perhaps he is in love with the victim's wife or he is burning for revenge. The action of a murderer is wrong, but he has a reason for committing his crime. Augustine understands the reason he indulged in sexual sins; he did so out of lust and desire for pleasure. Yet the theft of the pears is a serious puzzle to him because it was a senseless crime; it does not seem to have an understandable motive. So he asks himself, "What did I love in you? O theft, what did I love in you, the nocturnal crime of my sixteenth year. There was nothing beautiful about you, for you were nothing but a theft. Are you really anything at all, for me to be speaking to you like this?" (*Conf.* II.6.12). Before we address this issue, notice how Augustine has changed his question. Instead of asking, "What was I seeking in my sin?" or "Why did I do it?" he now asks, "What did I *love* in this sinful

---

5. Augustine does give motives for his behavior but he is not satisfied with them, so he continues his inquiry to find a deeper, more satisfying answer.

action?" In other words, was there anything beautiful to love in his theft? The answer is no; Augustine says that there was nothing beautiful about his theft and that it was nothing but a theft. To drive home this point, he discusses several kinds of beauties to compare them to his theft:

> So now, Lord my God, when I ask what it was that gave me plea-sure in that theft, I find nothing of fair, seductive form at all. I do not mean simply that it lacked the beauty to be found in justice and prudence, or the beauty of the human mind and intelligence, or that of our senses and bodily life, or the beauty inherent in the stars, so lovely in their appointed places, or in the earth and the sea full of young life born there to replace the things that die. No, I mean more: my theft lacked even the sham, shadowy beauty with which even vice allures us.[6]

Augustine speaks of several grades of beauty and concludes that his theft cannot compare to any of them. Even in our vices, Augustine insists, there is a counterfeit beauty that can deceive us. Yet Augustine insists that his theft even lacked the sham, shadowy beauty of any vice we may have. In this sense he can call his theft of the pears "a nothing."

Augustine has more to say about vices and their counterfeit beauty that can deceive. He mentions fifteen vices (including pride and ambition, to name two) that have some beauty in them, but he insists that in compari-son to God they fall short. Nonetheless, when we allow these vices to turn us from God, we are in a sense imitating God, but in a perverse way. It ap-pears that Augustine is referring to himself here, for he asks: "With regard to my theft, then: what did I love in it, and in what sense did I imitate my Lord, even if only with vicious perversity?" (*Conf.* II.6.14).

Augustine responds to this question with another question,

> Did the pleasure I sought lie in breaking the law at least in that sneaky way, since I was unable to do so with any show of strength? Was I, in truth a prisoner, trying to simulate a crippled sort of freedom, attempting a shady parody of omnipotence by getting away with something forbidden? How like that servant of yours who fled from his Lord and hid in the shadows![7]

We can summarize Augustine's train of thought as follows: He propos-es several motives for his sin, none of which satisfy him. So he goes deeper to ask what he loved in this act. He describes various kinds of goods, only to

6. *Confessions*, II.6.12.

7. Ibid., II.6.14.

say that his sinful act had no good in it. But from this analysis he discovers that his sin, and perhaps all sins, can in some way be viewed as an attempt to imitate God, but in a perverted way. On this point, Scott MacDonald offers an excellent summation of Augustine's condition:

> In breaking God's law with impunity he has grasped at freedom and power (his direct object), in a way that attempts to be like God (his indirect object)—it is as if he were asserting "I can do whatever I want! Not even divine law can restrict what I do." But the freedom is sham—it is the shackled freedom of a prisoner who can move only as far as and only in the manner in which his shackles permit him to move. And the power he claims for himself is at best a dim likeness of omnipotence. The whole affair, Augustine suggests, is predicated on the illusion that in flouting God's law he is asserting or claiming for himself a kind of freedom and power that he does not and cannot possess. He acts as if he alone determines the limits of his actions. He thereby imitates omnipotent God perversely.[8]

Augustine suggests not only that he imitated God in his theft of the pears but also that he in some way can be compared to Adam in the garden of Eden, when he says: "How like that servant of yours who fled from his Lord and hid in the shadows!" Throughout his *Confessions*, Augustine views himself as the prodigal son in the Gospels who has rebelled against his father, is living in sin in a faraway land, and therefore is in need of his father's love, mercy, and forgiveness. Likewise, he alludes to Adam and suggests that the sin in the theft of the pears can be compared to Adam's sin in the garden. The terms of the comparison are as follows: just as Adam sinned in the garden and was found hiding from God because he was afraid and ashamed, even so has Augustine hidden himself and separated himself from God because of the shame that his sin causes him, and so he suffers a sense of separation from God, a separation that can be cured only by seeking God's forgiveness through his *Confessions*. Augustine says as much: "Let me love you, Lord, and give thanks to you and confess to your name, because you have forgiven my grave sins and wicked deeds. By your sheer grace and mercy you melted my sins away like ice" (*Conf.* II.7.15).

Before Augustine proceeds, however, he offers a word of caution to anyone who might disparage his sinful life:

---

8. MacDonald, "Petit Larceny," 60.

> If there is anyone whom you have called, who by responding to your summons has avoided those sins which he finds me remembering and confessing in my own life as he reads this, let him not mock me; for I have been healed by the same doctor who has granted him the grace not to fall ill, or at least to fall ill less seriously. Let such a person therefore love you just as much, or even more, on seeing that the same physician who rescued me from sinful diseases of such gravity has kept him immune.[9]

Augustine now returns to his theft of the pears with one last point he must raise. He poses a question that he has previously answered; but it seems he cannot let the issue go before he makes one last point:

> What fruit did I ever reap from those things which I now blush to remember, and especially from that theft in which I found nothing to love save the theft itself, wretch that I was? It was nothing, and by the very act of committing it I became more wretched still. And yet, as I recall my state of mind at the time, I would not have done it alone. It follows, then, that I also loved the camaraderie with my fellow-thieves. So it is not true to say that I loved nothing other than the theft? Ah, but it is true, because that gang-mentality too was nothing.[10]

After reading this comment, one might ask why Augustine seems to contradict himself and to go back and forth about what he loves or what motivated him in this sin. He now says it was the love of the group and its camaraderie that was the motive for his sin; he then says that this camaraderie was a nothing. But then he admits that he would not have done this sin without the urging of the gang, and then at once insists again that this gang-mentality was a nothing. I think that when readers of the *Confessions* try to make perfect sense of Augustine's discussion of the theft of pears, they do him an injustice. The point that Augustine is making by his indecisive language is that sin is illogical and cannot always be explained with neat answers. His final comment on the subject says as much: "Who can unravel this most snarled, knotty tangle?" (*Conf.* II.10.18).

Finally, I believe Augustine is touching on a universal truth here that can be understood by youth of all generations: the negative influence a group can have on an individual. Augustine calls this influence "an exceedingly unfriendly form of friendship" (*Conf.* II.10.18). We can only wonder

9. *Confessions*, II.7.15.
10. Ibid., II.8.16.

how many young men are now in prison for following their comrades into far more sinister things that stealing pears.[11] In fact most of us would admit that some of the stupid things we did as youth seemed "okay" then but make no sense now. Perhaps, like Augustine, we would be hard pressed to find a single acceptable motive for our actions. Augustine thus challenges us today to get our youth to profit from our mistakes. Reminding us of the stakes involved here, he concludes book II with a word of both praise and warning:

> O justice and innocence, fair and lovely, it is on you that I want to gaze with eyes that see purely and find satiety in never being sated. With you is rest and tranquil life. Whoever enters into you enters the joy of the Lord; there he will fear nothing and find his own supreme good in God who is supreme goodness. I slid away from you and wandered away, my God; far from your steadfastness I strayed in adolescence, and I became to myself a land of famine.[12]

11. I make this statement as a person who has worked with youth and young men in various capacities, where I have seen the influence of gangs and peer pressure.

12. *Confessions*, II.10.18.

DISCUSSION QUESTIONS FOR CHAPTER 2

1. Discuss Augustine's 16th year. What was his opinion of himself and why?

2. From what you read or did not read, what do you think of the relationship between Augustine and his father?

3. What can we gleam from Augustine's *Confessions* that might help young people talk honestly about sex today?

4. From what you read or did not read, what do you think of the relationship between Augustine and his mother?

5. What do you think about the advice his mother gave him regarding fornication and adultery?

6. How was God speaking to Augustine during this time in his life? Did he listen? Why or why not?

7. Discuss the circumstances of Augustine's theft of the pears and the agony he had over it.

8. What are the different angles that Augustine uses to try to understand the sin of the pears?

9. Why do you think the theft of the pears is a big deal to him? Can it tell us anything about our own sins or shortcomings today?

10. Discuss how important friendship is to Augustine. How about what he calls camaraderie and how it can influence young people?

11. What is Augustine's point about vices? Do you agree or disagree?

12. What does Augustine have to say to those who might criticize his sinful life?

3

College Days at Carthage

DURING THE EARLY FIFTH century, Carthage was a thriving city that rivaled Alexandria in its claim to be the second city within the Roman Empire. As such, it had a large population of both Christian and pagan residents, wonderful entertainment, and outstanding educational opportunities for those who could afford them. Augustine informs us in book II that his father kept him home for a year so that he could save enough money to send him to Carthage to further his education. Well, Augustine has arrived in Carthage, and he describes the situation as follows:

> So I arrived at Carthage, where the din of scandalous love-affairs raged cauldron-like around me. I was not yet in love, but I was enamored with the idea of love, and so deep within me was my need that I hated myself for the sluggishness of my desires. In love with loving, I was casting about for something to love; the security of a way of life free from pitfalls seemed abhorrent to me, because I was inwardly starved of that food which is yourself, O my God. Yet this inner famine created no pangs of hunger in me. I had no desire for the food that does not perish, not because I had my fill of it, but because the more empty I was, the more I turned from it in revulsion.[1]

In some ways, Carthage was not unlike many of our college towns today where young students can learn from top-notch professors and experience freedom from parental authority. Of course this freedom is not

---

1. *Confessions*, III.1.1.

always used wisely; young Augustine used his free time to continue his sexual exploits and frequent the popular shows of his day. As he looks back on his behavior, Augustine is very self-critical; he says that he was in "love with love" and starving spiritually. Yet the statement just quoted reveals that Augustine now knows why his condition was so pitiful; it was that he lacked a relationship with God: "I was inwardly starved of that food which is you." As a result, Augustine goes on to say, his soul was in poor health, he had a kind of hellish lust, and he was vain and his way of living disgraceful. One might ask why Augustine was so hard on his youthful transgressions. At the time of this writing, Augustine is the bishop and pastor of a church in Hippo. He has rejected his past life to become a celibate priest. From his new vantage point, his old life looks disgusting. Consequently, Augustine needs to speak this harsh truth as he confesses his sins to God in hopes that he may bring healing to his own soul and perhaps help others at the same time.

In trying to understand his actions, Augustine told us in book II how he was influenced by the literature he read describing the sinful behavior of various gods. He now analyzes the influence the theatrical shows had on his life: "I was held spellbound by theatrical shows full of images that mirrored my own wretched plight and further fueled the fire within me" (*Conf.* III.2.2). Augustine is now aware how images entering through our senses can influence us deeply. Spellbound by these shows, he enjoyed being made sad by the drama he witnessed on stage: "In the capacity of spectator one welcomes sad feelings; in fact the sadness itself is a pleasure" (*Conf.* III.2.2). Consequently, if an actor did not move Augustine to tears, he considered it a bad performance. To all this Augustine now says, "What incredible stupidity!" He asks why being made sad by a theatrical performance was such a pleasure for him and for others even though they did not want to be sad in their own lives. Can it be, Augustine reasons (*Conf.* III.2.3), that everyone wants to be seen as being merciful, and mercy entails some sorrow? Following this line of reasoning, Augustine sees a danger when these emotions of sadness go unchecked:

> To be sure, this power of sympathy derives from the stream of friendship. But where does it flow to, whither is it bound? Why does it debouch into a torrent of boiling pitch, into seething passions of monstrous lust, so that it loses itself in them, is diverted and thrown off course, and deviates by its own choice from its heavenly serenity? Is mercy, then, to be rejected? By no means; it is sometimes right to entertain compassionate feelings. But beware

of impurity, my soul: under the guardianship of God, the God of our fathers who is to be praised and most highly exalted forever, beware of impurity.[2]

Augustine goes on to say that currently he is not devoid of merciful sensibilities but that as a youth his emotions were out of control. Augustine recognizes that our emotions can get out of control to the point where they bring forth evil that must be avoided.[3] In fact, for Augustine it appears that the shows held such influence over him that they not only wounded his character but had even become an addiction:

> At that time I was truly miserable, for I loved feeling sad and sought out whatever could cause me sadness. When the theme of a play dealt with other people's tragedies—false and theatrical tragedies—it would please and attract me more powerfully the more it moved me to tears. I was an unhappy beast astray from your flock and resentful of your shepherding, so what wonder was it that I became infected with foul mange? My love for tragic scenes sprang from no inclination to be more deeply wounded by them, for I had no desire to undergo myself the woes I liked to watch. It was simply that when I listened to such doleful tales being told they enabled me superficially to scrape away at my itching self, with the result that these raking nails raised an inflamed swelling, and drew stinking discharge from a festering wound. Was that life I led any life at all, O my God?[4]

Augustine compares this period in his life to the story of the lost sheep in the gospel narrative and so concludes this section with the question, "Was that life I led any life at all, O my God"? And the answer implied by this question is that it was not much of a life, because it was a life dominated by his flesh and his emotions.

In section 3.6 of book III, Augustine discusses the reason for which he came to Carthage in the first place: to further his education. In spite of his extra-curricular activities, Augustine was in fact the best student in the school of rhetoric, though he admits that this caused him to become vain and prideful. Nonetheless, Augustine informs us, he did avoid some group mischief. At age sixteen, he had been influenced into stealing pears for no

---

2. Ibid., III.2.3.

3. In Augustine's view, only God can show mercy in a pure way, in which sorrow does not wound his character.

4. *Confessions*, III.2.4.

good reason, except for the camaraderie of it. In Carthage, however, he avoided a more sinister group called the "wreckers." They were upperclassmen who took it upon themselves to seek out the lowerclassmen for abuse. Augustine tells us that "they would chase sensitive freshmen relentlessly, taunting and hounding them on no provocation, simply for their own malicious amusement" (*Conf.* III.3.6). This too recalls incidents at some of our college campuses today, where new initiates of fraternities often suffer unreasonable abuse. On this score, at least, Augustine is happy to say he avoided being influenced by them or taking part in their evil behavior, even though he did occasionally associate with them.

In section 4.7 of book III, Augustine returns to a discussion of his studies. He recalls how a reading of Cicero's work *Hortensius* changed his life profoundly; Augustine insists that it was the contents of this book that moved him to fall in love with philosophy and become a seeker of wisdom. As a seeker of wisdom, Augustine turned to the Bible to see what it had to say to him. Yet after having read Cicero and other Latin writers, he found the lack of polish within the pages of these Scriptures crude. Thus, in his arrogance, he rejected Scripture. Looking back, Augustine now recalls his unwillingness to receive God's word in humility:

> My approach then was quite different from the one I am suggesting now: when I studied the Bible and compared it with Cicero's dignified prose, it seemed to me unworthy. My swollen pride recoiled from its style and my intelligence failed to penetrate to its inner meaning. Scripture is a reality that grows along with little children, but I disdained to be a little child and in my high and mighty arrogance regarded myself as grown up.[5]

In reaction to his disappointment with Christian Scripture, Augustine joined the sect of the Manichaeans. Mani, the founder of Manichaeism, was born in Babylonia (now modern Iran) in the early third century. At age twenty-four, Mani received what he believed to be a heavenly order to proclaim his new doctrine. He was obedient to the vision and began proclaiming his teaching with much initial success. Soon, however, he was persecuted and eventually martyred around 274–277 CE. Before he died, however, he was able to record his teaching in several books that his followers continued to propagate. They succeeded in spreading Manichaeism throughout Persia and eventually throughout the entire Roman Empire.

---

5. Ibid., III.5.9.

Within twenty years of Mani's death Manichaeism had reached Alexandria and shortly afterward the whole of North Africa.

Some scholars have described Manichaeism as a Christian heresy, but its teaching is closer to Gnosticism in many respects than to that of its Christian rival. For example, the Manichaeans did not accept the virgin birth or the crucifixion of Jesus Christ.[6] Nor did they accept the belief that God became man to redeem humankind. They also rejected the God of the Old Testament and the account of creation as recorded in Genesis. In addition to rejecting the entire Old Testament, they also rejected much of the New. They did, however, accept some passages in the New Testament. For example, Paul's statements in Romans 7:23 and 8:7 were accepted, because these verses seemed to support their teaching regarding the tension between good and evil. Many other texts, however, particularly in the gospels, were targets of their criticism, because of apparent discrepancies between the different gospels. For example, Matthew "says there are three groups of fourteen generations between Christ and Abraham, but he gives in fact in his account only forty-one, that is, one less."[7] They did speak of God, Jesus, and the Holy Spirit, but in ways quite different from Christianity. For example, Mani taught that the Holy Spirit resided in him personally, so as to imply that he was divine himself (*Conf.* V.5.8). The Manichaeans were dualists who believed in the forces of both good and evil; they saw the world as a battleground between the kingdom of light and the kingdom of darkness. However, their god of light was not omnipotent, but was limited by evil forces (demons) that controlled the kingdom of darkness. This teaching allowed them to explain how evil existed in the world and in their personal lives. In addition, at the core of their belief system was the teaching that men and women have an evil body in which their soul is held captive. This captive soul can be freed from the body only by special knowledge. Thus, salvation is brought about by a special knowledge (*gnosis*).[8] On this point, they agreed with other gnostic sects, but not with basic Christian doctrine. At the time of Augustine's admission to the group, there were three issues that drew him into the movement. He recalls this quite clearly:

> The trouble was that I knew nothing else; I did not recognize the other, true reality. I was being subtly maneuvered into accepting the views of those stupid deceivers by the questions they

6. O'Meara, *Young Augustine*, 55.

7. Ibid.

8. Ibid., 61.

constantly asked me about the origin of evil, and whether God was confined to a material form with hair and nails, and whether people who practiced polygamy, killed human beings and offered animal sacrifices could be considered righteous. Being ignorant of these matters I was very disturbed by the questions, and supposed that I was approaching the truth when I was in fact moving away from it.[9]

Let us address the three issues Augustine cites above: (1) the problem of evil, (2) the anthropomorphic conceptions of God, and (3) the lives of the Old Testament saints. In section 3.7 of book III, it is important to note that Augustine says several times that he did not know or recognize the true reality.[10] At the time he fell in love with wisdom, his knowledge of Christianity was minimal, at best. Consequently, when the Manichaeans repeatedly asked him to give answers to questions that stumped him, his superficial knowledge of Christian doctrine was destroyed. But why did those three questions cause him and other Christians who joined the Manichaeans at the time so much grief? Partly because many Christians could not harmonize their understanding of an omnipotent God with the existence of evil in the world. Specifically, why did bad things happen to good people, if God was all-powerful? The Manichaean would say that this happened because there were two forces, good and evil, in the world, and the evil force prevented the good force from having its way. So in their system God was not omnipotent but subject to challenges from an opposing and apparently equal force. This seemed reasonable to Augustine at the time so he joined their group. Augustine would later find a way to defeat this teaching by insisting that evil is not a substance, but only the "diminishment of good to the point where nothing at all is left" (*Conf.* III.7.12).[11]

Regarding the anthropomorphic view of God, the Manichaeans taught that, since Christian Scriptures said that man is made in the image of God, then the Christian God must have a human body, with hair, nails, feet, etc. This caused Augustine to turn away from the Christian God, because, in his view, any being with a physical body was limited in a way that God could not be limited. Even though he did not know how to think of God at the time, he did believe that God was not subject to a human, physical body, as

9. *Confessions*, III.7.12.

10. The Latin text insists quite strongly that at the time, Augustine did not know what was true: "Nesciebam enim aliud vere quod est."

11. Augustine will address the problem of evil more fully in book VII of his *Confessions*.

he believed was taught by the Catholic Church. Augustine finally overcame this problem when he heard the preaching of Ambrose, who taught that God is a spiritual being with a spiritual body and so corrected Augustine's misapprehension of Catholic teaching.

Lastly, the Manichaeans were also very adept at attacking the lifestyles of the Old Testament patriarchs. They criticized their proclivity to violence, their practice of polygamy, and their animal sacrifices to demonstrate that they were not righteous men and women.[12] Again, at the time this seemed reasonable to Augustine, but by the time he wrote the *Confessions* he maintained that God allowed certain laws and behavior in one period that were prohibited in another. Additionally, once Augustine left the Manichaeans, he came to realize that they had much more extreme and fanciful teaching than that of the Catholic Church. Augustine recalls this in vivid detail:

> Little by little, I was being lured into such absurdities as the belief that a fig wept when plucked, and its mother tree too wept milky tears. Then, I was told, if one of the saints ate the fig (plucked, of course, not by any fault on his part but by someone else's), it would be absorbed by his digestive system and then when he belched or groaned in prayer he would spew out angels, or even particles of God. These particles of God most high, of the true God, would have remained trapped in the fruit unless liberated by the teeth and belly of one of the holy elect! I believed, poor wretch, that it was accordingly a higher duty to show mercy to the fruits of the earth than to human beings, for whom they came into existence; for if some hungry person who was not a Manichee asked for one, it was believed that to give it to him entailed passing a death-sentence on that morsel.[13]

When we understand that the Manichaeans believed that divine life existed in everything, we can understand better what Augustine is stating above. Because the divine was in everything, an "Elect" Manichaean—the highest rank within the Manichaean community—would not pluck a fig or cut a weed, nor would he take a bath because it would tear the divine substance in the water.[14] Other Manichaeans ("Hearers") had to bring the Elect their food, but the Hearers could not give this food to anyone else. This is the basis for Augustine's statement that according to Manichaeism

---

12. O'Meara, *Young Augustine*, 53.

13. *Confessions*, III.10.18.

14. O'Meara, *Young Augustine*, 64.

it was a higher duty to show mercy to fruit than to people that were not Manichaeans. He now sees this as absurd.[15]

In his *Confessions* and in other writings, Augustine expresses his anger with himself for believing the lies of the Manichaeans for so long.[16] Consequently, we must also be mindful of Augustine's evangelistic aims in his *Confessions*. Many of Augustine's answers to Manichaeism are written to inform Manichaean readers of their error. When he was a Hearer for the Manichaeans he used his rhetorical skills to win Christians over to Manichaeism; now as a Christian he is trying to win some of them back to the fold, which he did with much success.[17]

In closing out book III, Augustine relates how his mother was so upset with him becoming a Manichaean that she did not want to live with him. But now he sees this as an opportunity to praise God, for when he thought God was silent, God was actually speaking through his mother:

> You stretched out your hand from on high and pulled my soul out of these murky depths because my mother, who was faithful to you, was weeping for me more bitterly than ever mothers wept for the bodily death of their children. In her faith and in the spiritual discernment she possessed by your gift she regarded me as dead; and you heard her, O Lord, you heard her and did not scorn those tears of hers which gushed forth and watered the ground beneath her eyes wherever she prayed. Yes, you did indeed hear her, for how else can I account for the dream by which you so comforted her that she agreed to live with me and share my table, under the same roof?[18]

Augustine's account of his mother's reaction to his embrace of Manichaeism makes clear that African Christians did not have a favorable view of that religious system.[19] But two events happened that allowed his mother to tolerate his new religion. First, she was given a heavenly dream

---

15. This is also, the reason why most Manichaeans did not climb the ranks to become Elect but remained, as Augustine did, a "Hearer."

16. Regarding his anger, he writes: "I felt bitterly angry with the Manichees, though my indignation was tinged with pity, because they knew nothing of this remedy and ranted against the very antidote which might have healed them" (*Conf.* IX.4.8).

17. Augustine did in fact win some of his friends over to Christianity. The Donatists noted this and were quick to criticize him for it. See Burris, *Where Is the Church*, 115–16.

18. *Confessions*, III.11.19.

19. The Donatist Christians had an even less favorable view of Manichaeism than their Catholic counterparts.

that revealed that Augustine would eventually be saved before she died. Second, her local priest encouraged her by saying, "It is inconceivable that he should perish, a son of tears like yours" (*Conf.* III.12.21). She took those words at if God spoke them directly to her. From that point forward Monnica would never waver in her belief that her son would be saved before she departed this life.

DISCUSSION QUESTIONS FOR CHAPTER 3

1. Describe Augustine's experience at school in Carthage. Was his experience similar to college students today?

2. Why was Augustine so critical of his youthful indiscretions?

3. Discuss the theatrical shows and their influence on Augustine. Is Augustine ahead of his time in pointing this out or is he making excuses for his behavior?

4. Were the theatrical shows an addiction for Augustine? Or is this too strong a word?

5. Why did Augustine ask, "Was that life I led any life at all, O my God?"

6. How did Cicero's work *Hortensius* affect Augustine?

7. Discuss the teaching of Mani or Manichaeism as noted in chapter three. How does it compare to the teaching of Christianity?

8. What were the three issues that drew Augustine to Manichaeism? Are those issues relevant today? Why or why not?

9. What was the difference between the Elect and the Hearers among the Manichaeans?

10. How did Monnica feel about Augustine becoming a Manichaean? Does this tell us anything about how Manichaeism might have been viewed among African Christians?

11. What did God do to comfort Monnica's heart and mind when Augustine became a Manichaean?

12. What did Monnica's local priest do and say to comfort her heart and mind?

4

Adulthood (19–29)

In book IV, Augustine describes the period in his life from age nineteen to twenty-nine, during which he was a "Hearer" with the sect of the Manichaeans. As he looks back on these years, he is very critical of his spiritual condition. He believes himself to have been very superstitious. He is also critical of his educational pursuits because he believes he was too arrogant. He does, however, have at least two positive things to say about himself. First, he was a dedicated teacher and did his best to teach his students with integrity (*Conf.* IV.2.2). Second, Augustine informs us that at this time in his life he had a live-in girlfriend who was basically his wife, yet without the legal title or status that a legitimate marriage would have afforded her. Nonetheless, they lived together as a loving couple, raised a child together, and were sexually faithful to one another during their time together. It appears that Augustine began this live-in relationship at the age of eighteen or nineteen. So for all of his criticism of his previous lustful behavior, his yielding to unbridled lust ended when this relationship began; for the next fourteen or so years he lived a respectable and respectful life with his mistress and child. Augustine does not speak much about his son in book IV, but it is likely that his son is one of the babies he observes sinning and being angry in book I. We also know that Augustine's father was excited about the prospects of being a grandfather, but it appears that he died before the birth of his grandson (*Conf.* II.3.6). Moreover, when his mother agreed to live with him (after being given a dream that one day he would be saved) she probably did so with the thought of helping raise her grandson as well as helping manage the household.

After this brief mention of his family, Augustine recounts a dramatic poetry contest he entered while teaching in Thagaste. What is interesting about this contest is that one of the local sorcerers assured Augustine he could help him win the contest if he would solicit his services. In response to this offer, Augustine informs us of his extreme dislike for this profession. He says that he would not allow the killing of a fly to bring him the victory, even if the crown to be won were of gold that would last forever (*Conf.* IV.2.3). Augustine won the contest on his own ability, but in recalling this incident, he now sees himself in the same position in which he had previously seen the sorcerer:

> Yet while refusing to have sacrifice offered to demons on my behalf I was all the while offering myself in sacrifice to them through my superstition; for what does "feeding the winds" mean but feeding demons, providing pleasure and amusement for them by our errors?[1]

In looking back on his life, Augustine is very self-critical, but he is also sympathetic to his former self because he admits that he had not yet learned to love God and to view God in a way that would allow him to accept God. Augustine's point is that persons who may read his *Confessions* may also find hope in their situation if they will turn to God and away from vain things.

One theme that Augustine revisits throughout his *Confessions* is the fact that God was not silent during his time of wandering. When Augustine was fascinated by the mathematicians and astrologers of his day, he recalls how an older man gave him fatherly advice:

> Were you deserting me, or giving up the task of curing my soul? No; even through that old man you were at work. It happened like this. I had become quite well known to him, and listened regularly and attentively to his speeches, for although unpolished in style they were pleasant to the ear and weighty for the vigorous ideas they expressed. Through conversation with me he learned that I was deeply interested in the writings of those who professed to cast birth horoscopes. In kindly and fatherly fashion he advised me to throw them away, and not to waste on such rubbish the care and effort better spent on more useful enterprises. He told me that

1. *Confessions*, IV.2.3.

as a young man he had learned astrology with such zeal that he had wanted to make it his career and earn his living by it. If he had the intelligence to understand Hippocrates, he pointed out, he was certainly capable of mastering those books. Later, however, he abandoned them and took up medicine, for no other reason than that he had discovered them to be entirely misleading, and as an honorable man he did not want to make his living by deceiving others. "But you," he said, "you can support yourself and maintain your social position by the profession of rhetoric, so you are pursuing this fraudulent study as a hobby, not from any economic necessity. All the more reason, then, for you to believe me when I inform you about this subject in which I was so well versed myself that I meant to make my living by it alone."[2]

After this admonition, Augustine went on to ask the man how it is that astrologers make predictions that seem to be true. In a convincing manner, the wise man told Augustine that many times this is due to chance and the fact that people often read into things what they want to hear. Augustine, however, did not immediately give up astrology; but the wise man had planted a seed that would later allow him to seek and validate for himself the falsehood of this profession. Again, God was speaking to Augustine, but he could not comprehend that reality at the time.

In sections 4.7 to 7.12 of book IV, Augustine goes into great detail concerning the death of a friend. Throughout Augustine's life, friends as well as family members surround him. Yet the death of his own father is passed over in book II with little attention. Then, at twenty-one years of age, he is devastated by the death of a close friend. In recalling the incident, Augustine gives us the following details: he knew this friend since childhood, they were the same age and went to school together as children. Moreover, as young adults they became close friends, and Augustine was able to convince him to leave the Catholic faith and become a "Hearer" in the Manichaean faith, like himself. At the time Augustine described their relationship as "one soul in two bodies" (*Conf.* IV.6.11).[3] But, unfortunately,

---

2. Ibid., IV.3.5.

3. In his *Revisions* (*Retractiones*), a reconsideration of his works written late in his life, Augustine would later criticize this characterization of their relationship. In his words, "In the fourth book, after I confessed the misery of my soul on the death of a friend, saying that in some way our soul had been made one from two, I say: 'And perhaps I was so afraid of death because I did not want the whole of him to die, whom I had loved so dearly.' This seems to me, as it were, a trifling pronouncement rather than a serious confession, although this absurdity may be moderated to some extent by the word 'perhaps'

his close friend suddenly became gravely ill. His family, fearing the worst, had him baptized while he was unconscious. His friend was unaware of the baptism at the time but accepted it when he came to his senses. During his brief period of recovery, Augustine attempted to criticize his Christian baptism, at which his friend not only rebuked him but also told him if he wanted to continue being his friend he had better stop speaking to him in that manner. Augustine was shocked by his friend's newfound independence and his acceptance of Christian baptism. Perhaps Augustine was shocked to find that he did not have as much influence over his friend as he thought. Yet Augustine, as he recalls, was determined to speak with him again on this matter once he had fully recovered. This never happened, because his friend became sick again and died suddenly without Augustine having the opportunity to speak to him again. Devastated by the sudden death of his friend, Augustine was inconsolable. In recalling the situation Augustine says:

> Black grief closed over my heart and wherever I looked I saw only death. My native land was a torment to me and my father's house unbelievable misery. Everything I had shared with my friend turned into hideous anguish without him. My eyes sought him everywhere, but he was missing; I hated all things because they held him not, and could no more say to me, "Look, here he comes!" as they had been wont to do in his lifetime when he had been away. I had become a great enigma to myself, and I questioned my soul, demanding why it was sorrowful and why it so disquieted me, but it had no answer.[4]

Augustine describes here the loss of a friend at a time in which his religious faith (Manichaeism) did not appear to offer him much comfort. Indeed, his friend had left his Manichaean faith before he died and accepted the baptism of the Catholic Church—something Augustine could not appreciate at the time. Upon retelling this story, Augustine admits that what helped him get over this loss was tears, the joy of other friends, leaving his place of birth, and time. But as he looks back on this incident Augustine is also curious about the process of grieving and so he asks, "Let me listen now to you who are truth; bring the ear of my heart close to your mouth, that you may tell me why weeping is a relief to the wretched" (*Conf.* IV.5.10). Augustine proceeds to suggest several answers to this question and rejects

which I added." *Revisions*, II.6.32.

4. *Confessions*, IV.4.9.

them all. But he goes on to note several things that he has learned from his grieving. First, he realizes that he loved his friend in such a way that his actions were inappropriate. He says, "I had poured out my soul into the sand by loving a man doomed to death as though he were never to die" (*Conf.* IV.8.13). Loving his friend was not the problem, but loving him as if he would live forever was inappropriate. Augustine also sees a problem in the comfort he sought from his friends: "What restored and re-created me above all was the consolation of other friends, in whose company I loved what I was loving as a substitute for God" (*Conf.* IV.8.13). The last phrase tells us what problem Augustine saw in this, and he offers us some advice worth considering. First, we can love people, but in loving them, we must realize that they (like ourselves) will die, and we cannot prevent that from happening. Second, if we love God first and then love our friends in God—the one who is never lost—we still have hope because we trust that one day we will see them again. This is why Augustine believes that the true consolation we must seek, even above that offered by our friends, is found in God, the giver of all life (*Conf.* IV.9.14). So the believer, in this sense, has no loss in God.

In section 10.15 of book IV, Augustine connects the loss of his friend and other temporal things with the need to praise God, because God has set certain laws in operation as it pleases him:

> Turn us toward yourself, O God of Hosts, show us your face and we shall be saved, for wheresoever a human soul turns, it can but cling to what brings sorrow unless it turns to you, cling though it may to beautiful things outside you and outside itself. Yet were these beautiful things not from you, none of them would be at all. They arise and sink; in their rising they begin to exist and grow toward their perfection, but once perfect they grow old and perish; or, if not all reach old age, yet certainly all perish. So then, even as they arise and stretch out toward existence, the more quickly they grow and strive to be, the more swiftly they are hastening toward extinction. This is the law of their nature.[5]

Since God has ordered things to exist for a while and then perish, we should enjoy the things created by God (including people), but with a proper perspective. Again, to drive home his point regarding temporal things, Augustine connects things that pass away with our audible speech. That is, just as things begin to exist and then pass away, so it is with our

5. Ibid., IV.10.15.

speech. One word is spoken, and then it dies so that the next word may be spoken. And since this is true, Augustine offers the following praise for our consideration:

> Let my soul use these things to praise you
> O God, creator of them all,
> but let it not be glued fast to them by sensual love,
> for they are going whither they were always destined to go,
> toward extinction;
> and they rend my soul with death-dealing desires,
> for it too longs to be, and loves to rest in what it loves.
> But in them it finds no place to rest,
> because they do not stand firm;
> they are transient, and who can follow them with the senses of the body?
> Or who can seize them, even near at hand?
> Tardy is carnal perception, because it is carnal;
> such is the law of its nature.
> Sufficient it is for another purpose, for which it was made,
> but insufficient to catch the fleeting things
> that rush past from their appointed beginning
> to their appointed end.
> In your Word, through whom they are created,
> they hear your command,
> "From here begin, and thus far you shall go."[6]

The death of Augustine's friend at twenty-one was a powerful and emotional event in his life. Moreover, it was an event that he could not handle well at that time in his life because he had neither the proper perspective on life nor a relationship with God. He now realizes all temporal things (including people) will move toward extinction. That is why he can now say that we should praise God for these things (like his deceased friend) but not hold to them as if they will last forever, for they will not. And in the third line of his statement above, he speaks of other fleeting relationships; for he says, "Let us not be glued to them in sensual love, because they too are going toward extinction." But if those things (beauty, sensual love, people) excite us, let us praise God for what is pleasing in them, lest the thing that pleases us cause us to not please God (*Conf.* IV.12.18). Augustine is challenging us to put the creator above creation and give God the praise for whatever is beautiful in creation. Augustine closes out this section with a return to his theme of "rest." He asks:

6. Ibid.

> Tell me, where are you going? The good which you love derives from him, and insofar as it is referred to him it is truly good and sweet, but anything that comes from him will justly turn bitter if it is unjustly loved by people who forsake him. Why persist in walking difficult and toilsome paths? There is no repose where you are seeking it. Search as you like, it is not where you are looking. You are seeking a happy life in the realm of death, and it will not be found there. How could life be happy, where there is no life at all?[7]

Augustine is surely speaking of his own past experience when he asks how life could be happy where there is no life at all. He realizes how much time he wasted in vain things, seeking happiness where it could not be found. But now he is certain where happiness can be found. Happiness and true beauty can be found in the second person of the Trinity. So he declares in a sermonic exhortation the truth about Christ:

> He who is our very life came down, and took our death upon himself. He slew our death by his abundant life and summoned us in a voice of thunder to return to him in his hidden place, that place from which he set out to come to us when first he entered the Virgin's womb. There a human creature, mortal flesh, was wedded to him that I might not remain mortal forever; and from there he came forth like a bridegroom from his nuptial chamber, leaping with joy like a giant to run his course. Impatient of delay he ran, shouting by his words, his deeds, his death and his life, his descent to hell and his ascension to heaven, shouting his demand that we return to him. Then he withdrew from our sight, so that we might return to our own hearts and find him there.[8]

At the conclusion of this exhortation, Augustine admits that he was ignorant of this gospel message that he is now speaking about, for he was in love with beautiful things below himself (*Conf.* IV.13.20). So Augustine begins to examine beauty and the reasons why people are attracted to it. He remembers that around the age of twenty-six or twenty-seven, he wrote several books entitled *The Beautiful and the Harmonious*. Those books were lost by the time he wrote his *Confessions*, but Augustine remembers that he dedicated those books to an orator named Hierius and that he dedicated those books to him because he was a Syrian who was highly esteemed by others for his knowledge of Greek and Latin literature. Moreover, Augustine wanted to be like him because he received praise from people he

7. Ibid., IV.12.18.
8. Ibid., IV.12.19.

respected. In looking back on this, however, Augustine is bothered by what really motivated him to dedicate those books to Hierius:

> How did I know, how can I confess to you with such certainty, that I had come to love him more for the love he aroused in those who sang his praises than for the achievement by which he won them? I know because if, instead of praising him, those same people had recounted his deeds with disparagement and contempt, I would not have warmed to him or felt any interest; and yet neither the facts nor the man himself would have been different; the difference would have lain only in the attitude of those who related them.[9]

Augustine is thinking about the influence we allow people to have over us. Now in the case of Hierius, the praise he received was well deserved. However, Augustine is troubled because he knows that if this same man had been criticized by the same people that praised him, he would not have held him in high esteem—even though he would have been just as worthy of respect and praise. Augustine now views his past behavior as prideful. For at the heart of his appreciation of Hierius was his desire to have people feed his ego by praising him, as they did Hierius, so he could feel important in their eyes. This desire for praise can also influence how we view ourselves. For example, Augustine also recalls that, although he thought his books were good, he would have been sad if Hierius had criticized his books and happy had Hierius approved them. Augustine's point is that we cannot rightly judge what is good or beautiful if we are influenced by the praise of people rather than by truth. Beauty must somehow be viewed from God's perspective, and we must first of all seek Christ, the one who died that we might live.

In the first three books of his *Confessions*, Augustine is very critical of his sexual exploits and his outward sins (such as stealing pears); in much of book IV, however, Augustine is looking inward. He is examining the thoughts and misperceptions he had about God. For example, Augustine now admits that his misguided views about God and his prideful thinking about himself in relation to God caused him to walk in darkness when he thought he was walking in the light. Augustine speaks candidly of his past condition:

> What could be prouder than my outlandish delusion, whereby I laid claim to be by nature what you are? I was subject to change, as was obvious to me from the fact that I was clearly seeking to be

9. Ibid., IV.14.23.

wise in order to change for the better, yet I was prepared even to think you changeable than admit that I was not what you are.[10]

And, in regard to the supreme God and the forces of evil, Augustine has this to say:

> I was readier to assert that your immutable substance had been forced into error, than to confess that my own mutable substance had gone astray by its own will, and that its error was its punishment.[11]

One of the most important revelations for Augustine was the realization that God is immutable and not subject to any evil that happens in this world. For evil, in Augustine's view, is not a substance but merely the absence of good. Therefore, we sin because we chose to do so by our own will, not because God is subject to some evil force.[12]

In closing this book, Augustine finds God's grace in the following scenario. While he had sought much learning in a "plethora of intricate books," these books did not lead him into a relationship with God. Augustine in fact recalls how many "slow-minded persons" were in the church and growing stronger each day in their relationship with God. In the face of such wonderful workings of God, he ends book IV with a closing section of prayer and praise:

> O Lord our God
> grant us to trust in your overshadowing wings:
> protect us beneath them and bear us up.
> You will carry us as little children,
> and even to our grey-headed age you will carry us still.
> When you are our strong security, that is strength indeed,
> but when our security is in ourselves, that is but weakness.
> Our good abides ever in your keeping,
> but in diverting our steps from you we have grown perverse.
> Let us turn back to you at last, Lord, that we be not overturned.
> Unspoilt, our good abides with you,
> for you are yourself our good.
> We need not fear to find no home again
> because we have fallen away from it;

---

10. Ibid., IV.15.26.

11. Ibid.

12. Augustine goes into more detail about the problem of evil in book VII of his *Confessions*.

while we are absent our home falls not to ruins,
for our home is your eternity.[13]

---

13. *Confessions* IV.16.31.

DISCUSSION QUESTIONS FOR CHAPTER 4

1. What major change(s) happened in Augustine's life when he was 18 or 19?

2. Discuss Augustine's encounter with the sorcerer, and why did he later compare himself to the sorcerer whom he criticized?

3. Name at least one person God used in book IV to speak wisdom to Augustine.

4. What were the circumstances surrounding the death of Augustine's friend, and why do you think he grieved so hard?

5. What do you think about his friend's acceptance of the Christian baptism administered when he was unconscious? What was Augustine's response to the secret baptism of his friend?

6. What did Augustine learn about grieving from the death of his friend?

7. Why do you think Augustine grieved so hard over his friend, when he barely mentioned the death of his father in book II?

8. Discuss this quotation from Augustine: "Let my soul use these things to praise you, O God, creator of them all, but let it not be glued fast to them by sensual love, for they are going whither they were always destined to go, toward extinction."

9. Why did Augustine dedicate several books to Heirius the Syrian?

10. What was wrong with Augustine's motivation for this dedication? Do you disagree with Augustine's assessment of this?

11. What were Augustine's misguided views about God? How did they hinder him from coming to know God?

12. Discuss Augustine's view of evil and the Manichaean view of evil.

5

God's Hidden Providence

IN BOOK V, AUGUSTINE sounds a new theme: that God was leading him by his hidden and secret providence. Of course, Augustine could not see it at the time, but now that he is aware of God's providence, it causes him to break out in celebration and praise as he introduces book V:

> Accept the sacrifice of my confessions, offered to you by the power of this tongue of mine which you have fashioned and aroused to confess to your name; bring healing to all my bones and let them exclaim, *Lord, who is like you?* A person who confesses to you is not informing you about what goes on within him, for a closed heart does not shut you out, nor is your hand pushed away by human obduracy; you melt it when you choose, whether by showing mercy or by enforcing your claim, and from your fiery heat no one can hide.[1]

Augustine continues his praise until the end of section 2.2 before returning to his life's narrative in section 3.3. At the age of twenty-nine, Augustine had an encounter with the renowned Manichaean bishop Faustus that proved pivotal to his spiritual and intellectual development. The Manichaeans saw Faustus as one of their leading lights; whenever Augustine posed a difficult question to the group, they would assure him that his question would be answered once he had the opportunity to speak with Bishop Faustus. And since Augustine had many questions turning over in his mind, he looked forward to meeting this renowned speaker

1. *Confessions*, V.1.1.

44

with great anticipation. For Augustine informs us that he was beginning to have doubts about some elements of Manichaean belief even before he met Faustus. Because of his extensive reading, Augustine was able to compare certain elements from his reading with the "long-winded myths of the Manichaeans" (*Conf.* V.3.3). The result: Mani's teaching fell short of the mark. What Augustine had begun to feel were Mani's overblown claims to universal knowledge became a major problem for the young African. For example, the philosophers of his day were able to predict certain eclipses of the sun and the moon with such accuracy that they would occur on the day in which they were predicted—thus verifying the accuracy of their knowledge. On the other hand, the Manichaean leaders wanted their followers to believe many things about the world—including matters well beyond religious doctrine—without any proof or rational explanation. In fact, Mani claimed to be an expert on many things regarding the order of the universe. Augustine might have accepted Mani as a pious teacher if Mani had not insisted on speaking about scientific things he knew little about. This was Mani's undoing for Augustine. For Mani to have the audacity to teach about the sky, the stars, the sun, the moon, and many other topics, while making statements about them that Augustine knew to be false, demonstrated to Augustine that he was neither a knowledgeable teacher nor a pious religious leader (*Conf.* V.5.8). Augustine sees God's guidance in Mani's inflated claims: "It was providential that this man talked so much about scientific subjects, and got it wrong, because this gave people who truly studied them the chance to convince him of error; and then by implication his insight into other, more recondite matters could be clearly assessed."[2] For Mani not only claimed to have broad knowledge of the universe but also taught that the Holy Spirit "was with full authority present in him personally" (*Conf.* V.5.8). In other words, he wanted his followers to hold him up as divine or at least as more than an ordinary human. Augustine saw that the hollowness of his claims to natural knowledge belied his claims to supernatural inspiration.

In looking back on Mani's wild assertions about himself, Augustine compares his behavior with that of the Christians he is now teaching:

> When I hear one or other of my fellow Christians expressing a mistaken opinion arising from his ignorance in these fields, I regard with tolerance the person who entertains the notion. As long as he does not believe anything unseemly about you, O Lord, creator of

---

2. Ibid., V.5.8.

all things, I do not see that it does him any harm if he chances to be ignorant of the position or characteristics of a material creature. It does harm him, however, if he thinks his view forms an essential part of our doctrine and belief, and presumes to go on obstinately making assertions about what he does not know.[3]

The point of course, is that this is exactly what Mani did and what Augustine now sees as one of his many faults. He could not see this at the time, until he finally met Bishop Faustus, the one charged, no less, with answering his difficult questions.

The day finally came when Faustus arrived in Carthage, and Augustine's first impression of him was very positive. Bishop Faustus was a very good speaker, had a command of the language he used, and spoke better than other Manichaeans on the usual themes they often addressed. Moreover, he had a debate style that pleased Augustine, and his choice of words was appropriate to his thoughts—all things that Augustine, as a teacher of rhetoric, appreciated. In addition, Faustus was pleasant to look at, with a handsome face (*Conf.* V.6.10). For these reasons, Augustine was initially impressed with him, along with others who first heard him. Yet after several lectures, Augustine's opinion quickly changed. Faustus was an eloquent speaker, for sure, but he lacked any serious content in what he said. Augustine was a seeker of truth and he had waited (with patience) to receive truthful answers from Faustus, but he was sorely disappointed. Once he was able to speak with him one-on-one and hear that he was poorly informed on the subjects that concerned him most, he quickly realized that the Manichaean did not hold the truth that he was seeking:

> To be sure, he could have been ignorant about these and still had a grasp of religious truth, but only on condition of not being a Manichee. Their books are full of interminable myths concerning sky, stars, sun and moon, and it had been my earnest wish that by comparing these with the numerical calculations I had read elsewhere he would demonstrate to me that the phenomena in question could be more plausibly explained by the account given in Mani's books, or at least that an equally valid explanation could be found there; but now I no longer deemed him capable of explaining these things to me with any precision.[4]

3. Ibid., V.5.9.
4. Ibid., V.7.12.

When Augustine heard Faustus, it was apparent that he commanded neither the knowledge that Augustine was seeking nor the wisdom concerning the world that the Manichaeans were claiming to possess. Nonetheless, Augustine found Faustus to be a man worthy of commendation for his restraint and honesty. That Faustus would not attempt to answer questions that he was ignorant of endeared him to Augustine. Consequently, they began to spend much time together, but this time with their roles reversed: Augustine became the teacher and Faustus the student. When Faustus witnessed Augustine teaching his students, he wanted to participate. Augustine allowed him to attend his lectures and thus read with him various books that Faustus was interested in and other books that Augustine felt were appropriate to his ability. Again, Augustine sees God's providence in this encounter:

> Thus it came about that this Faustus, who was a death–trap for many, unwittingly and without intending it began to spring the trap in which I was caught, for thanks to your hidden providence, O my God, your hands did not let go of my soul.[5]

Augustine continues his examination of God's providence as he rethinks his motivations for leaving Carthage and coming to Rome. Augustine was disgusted with the behavior of his students in Carthage; they would disrupt classes and commit acts of violence (presumably against other students) that he found repulsive. Augustine's attitude on this point is an interesting foil to his complaints about the strict discipline he received as a young child: it appears that the students in Carthage would have benefited from such discipline. In any event, Augustine was not able to control these unruly students, and this caused him much grief. So much grief, in fact, that he was willing to leave Carthage for Rome when he heard that the students there were better behaved and more studious. He was also told that he could make a name for himself in the Imperial City. Thus, Augustine left his native region for a brighter future in Rome.

When Augustine arrived in Rome, however, more disappointment was waiting for him. It was true that the students in Rome were not rowdy like those in Carthage, but he found he had a worse problem to contend with: the students in Rome were dishonest. Many of them would gather in a group, attend a professor's class for an extended period, and then leave for another class to avoid paying the fees due to their instructor. What

---

5. Ibid., V.7.13.

Augustine had hoped would be a great opportunity proved a great disappointment. Unexpectedly, however, another opportunity again presented itself. Augustine had not been long in Rome when a letter arrived requesting the services of a master teacher of rhetoric for the city of Milan. The person selected for the position would be allowed to use the official post horses—a notable privilege in a time when transportation between cities, even in the highly settled Roman Empire, was uncomfortable and unreliable. This was an excellent opportunity for Augustine. And with the help of his Manichaean friends, who were influential in Rome, he was able to secure the position.

After two disappointing teaching experiences in Carthage and Rome, Augustine looked to Milan with great expectations. Fortunately, in Milan, Augustine met the great preacher and father figure Bishop Ambrose. At this point (*Conf.* V.13.23–4), he leaves off speaking about his teaching pursuits to speak about Ambrose. When Augustine had the opportunity to meet Ambrose, he was thoroughly impressed. Not only did Ambrose have a reputation for being a good man and an excellent preacher, but he was kind as well. Augustine says of him, "This man of God welcomed me with fatherly kindness and showed the charitable concern for my pilgrimage that befitted a bishop" (*Conf.* V.13.23). It was this kindness that initially drew Augustine to Ambrose, but as he heard him the bishop's great preaching ability began to work its way with him:

> With professional interest I listened to him conducting disputes before the people, but my intention was not the right one: I was assessing his eloquence to see whether it matched its reputation. I wished to ascertain whether the readiness of speech with which rumor credited him was really there, or something more, or less. I hung keenly upon his words, but cared little for their content, and indeed despised it, as I stood there delighting in the sweetness of his discourse. Though more learned than that of Faustus it was less light-hearted and beguiling; but such criticism concerns the style only, for with regard to the content there was no comparison. While Faustus would wander off into Manichean whimsy, this man was teaching about salvation in a thoroughly salutary way. But salvation is far from sinners, and a sinner I was at that time. Yet little by little, without knowing it, I was drawing near.[6]

---

6. Ibid., V.13.23.

Because Augustine was a master teacher of rhetoric, his initial response to the preaching of Ambrose was that of a teacher analyzing an assignment. Yet this soon changed as Ambrose and the words he was speaking drew Augustine near. In fact, Ambrose was exactly what Augustine needed. He did not know this at the time, but God knew it. So, in God's providence, Augustine was allowed to experience various trials in Carthage and Rome, that led him to the one man whom he could listen too with respect and admiration. And listen he did, every chance he got. Upon listening to Bishop Ambrose's preaching on a consistent basis, Augustine realized several things that he had not seriously considered before this time: (1) that Ambrose was indeed speaking the truth when he preached the gospel; (2) that the gospel could be presented in an intelligent and respectful manner; and (3) that many difficult Old Testament Scriptures, which caused him to stumble in the past when he read them only literally, could in fact be interpreted figuratively and so made to yield a much more acceptable sense (*Conf.* V.14.24). After listening and being moved by the preaching of Ambrose, Augustine left the Manichaean sect and resolved for a while to be a catechumen in the Catholic Church. Though Augustine was not yet fully convinced of the truth of Christianity, the seed had been planted. We shall chart its growth in the next few chapters.

In sum, Augustine's encounter with Ambrose proved a perfect example of the theme of God's providence that runs through book V; as Augustine writes, "Unknowingly I was led by you to him, so that through him I might be led, knowingly, to you" (*Conf.* V.13.23).

In closing book V, with its theme of God's providence and Augustine's awareness of this fact, it is only fitting that Augustine ends with a reflective acknowledgement of his sin in light of God's providence and mercy. As if pleading with sinners in his previous condition, Augustine challenges them with these penetrating words:

> Let them turn back, and seek you,
> for you do not forsake your creation
> as they have forsaken their creator.
> Let them only turn back,
> see! there you are in their hearts,
> in the hearts of all those who confess to you,
> who fling themselves into your arms
> and weep against your breast after their difficult journey,
> while you so easily will wipe away their tears.
> At this they weep the more,

yet even their laments are matter for joy,
because you, Lord, are not some human being of flesh and blood,
but the Lord who made them,
and now make them anew and comfort them.
And what of myself: where was I as I sought you? You were straight
ahead of me, but I had roamed away from myself and could not
find even myself, let alone you![7]

7. Ibid., V.2.2.

DISCUSSION QUESTIONS FOR CHAPTER 5

1. What were some of the concerns Augustine had with what he read in the books of Mani, the leader of Manichaeism?

2. Why did Augustine look forward to meeting Bishop Faustus?

3. Discuss Augustine's initial impression of Faustus.

4. What was Augustine's impression of Faustus after he had the opportunity to hear several of his lectures and speak with him one-on-one?

5. What does Augustine say about God's providence in book V? Have you had any similar experiences in your own life?

6. Discuss Augustine's teaching experience in both Carthage and Rome.

7. What did Augustine think about Ambrose's preaching and how did this change his view of Christianity?

8. What was Augustine's initial motivation for listening to Ambrose?

9. What questions do you have regarding book V that you would like to share with the group?

6

From Disappointment to Hope

IN THE BEGINNING OF book VI, Augustine offers up a prayer and praise that describes his life at this stage of his journey toward salvation. He would become a solid Christian one day, but that day was yet to come. Now, however, it seemed that God had forgotten him, that he was hopelessly lost ("sinking to the depth of the sea"), and truth continued to elude him. Regarding this dreadful condition, he offers up the following prayer:

> O you who have been my hope since my youth where were you when I sought you? How was it that you have gone so far away? Had you not created me and marked me out *from the four-footed beasts, and made me wiser than the birds in the sky*? Yet I was walking a dark and slippery path, searching for you outside myself and failing to find the God of my own heart. I had sunk to the depth of the sea, I lost all faith and despaired of ever finding the truth.[1]

Of course Augustine's prayer here is rhetorical, because he now knows that God has certainly made him wiser than the birds of the air and the four-footed beasts of land, but it depicts very well his feelings at this point in his life. Before coming to Milan, he had met the renowned bishop Faustus only to be sorely disappointed. Faustus was a nice person, to be sure, and a skillful speaker, but the contents of what he said proved sorely disappointing to Augustine. He could not answer Augustine's many questions nor make intelligible the many myths of the Manichaeans. As a result, Augustine gave up hope of making any progress in the group. Even though

1. *Confessions*, VI.1.1.

52

he did not immediately leave the Manichaean community, intellectually he had severed all ties with the teaching of Mani. Thus, his search for the truth was started afresh. Fortunately, what Augustine calls the providence of God brought him to Milan and to his encounter with Bishop Ambrose. From this encounter, that is, from hearing the constant preaching and teaching of Ambrose each week, his heart and mind were gradually opening up to the Christian Scriptures.

Shortly after his arrival in Milan, however, Monnica came to Milan to be with her son, just as she had left Carthage and followed Augustine to Rome. This time, Augustine had some good news to give her: he was no longer a Manichaean. Monnica was overjoyed to hear this, but not totally surprised, because she had remained steadfast in her belief that she would see him a Christian believer before she died.[2] This belief was founded on the dream she received from God. This good news motivated Monnica to pray even harder for Augustine's salvation. Attending church even more faithfully, she petitioned God on behalf of her son. Bishop Ambrose was so impressed by this faithfulness that when he saw Augustine, he told him how lucky he was to have a mother like Monnica. Monnica was likewise impressed with Bishop Ambrose, because it was through his preaching that Augustine was beginning to more toward her faith. Augustine says she revered Ambrose as an angel of God (*Conf.* VI.1.1).

On one occasion, however, Bishop Ambrose felt compelled to rebuke this faithful woman of God. To Monnica's surprise, the practice of honoring the martyrs in Milan was different from that in Africa. In her native region, on the day of the martyrs' martyrdom believers would go to their tombs and celebrate the Eucharist. This was done as a way to both remember and honor the sacrifices made by the martyrs. In addition, African (and other) Christians believed that the martyrs' tombs and shrines were places of power where they could receive favors from God, such as healing. However, some believers would abuse this tradition by drinking too much at the tombs and thereby bringing a reproach upon other Christians. Augustine is well aware of this abuse but insists that his mother was not one of the abusers of this ritual. With what must have been an eyewitness account of her practice at the tombs, Augustine recalls:

2. "The translation offered here assumes the punctuation *sed neque catholicum christianum, non quasi inopinatum aliquid audierit, exilivit laetitia, cum iam secura.* Some editors of the Latin text place a comma after non, which would oblige us to understand that Monnica was not overjoyed, because she had expected the news." Boulding, trans., *Confessions*, 135.

With my mother it was otherwise: she would bring her basket containing the festive fare which it fell to her to taste first and then distribute; but she would then set out no more than one small cup, mixed to suit her abstemious palate, and from that she would only sip for courtesy's sake. If it happened that there were many shrines of the dead to be honored in this manner she would carry round this same single cup and set it forth in each place. She thus served to her fellow-worshippers extremely sparing allowances of wine which was not only heavily diluted but by this time no more than lukewarm. What she sought to promote at these gatherings was piety, not intemperance.[3]

In Milan, these practices were strictly forbidden, not only because of the abuses surrounding them but also because they closely resembled certain pagan practices. Monnica apparently was somewhat reluctant to give up the practices she had learned in Africa, but, because she held Ambrose in such high esteem, she quickly yielded to his rebuke and changed her custom to match that of Milan. Augustine marvels at this and believes that she would have complained, had it been anyone other than Ambrose who demanded this concession from her.

In section 3.3 of book VI, Augustine returns to his observation of Bishop Ambrose. Augustine had not met anyone, up to this point, who had the ability to make the Christian Scriptures palatable. Not only was Ambrose an excellent preacher, but he was also a loving pastor who attended to the needs of his people. Augustine, along with his mother, observed Ambrose working long hours as he met with crowds of people, who were allowed to see him unannounced. When Ambrose did have a moment to himself, Augustine found the bishop reading or eating something to refresh himself. Augustine wanted desperately to ask him questions, but he did not have the heart to disturb Ambrose during the little time the pastor had for himself. This was probably good for Augustine, however, because he was forced to listen carefully each Sunday to his sermons. Thus, instead of being able to present a list of questions to him, Augustine had to take the role of a student and absorb what was being taught. As a result, Augustine gained more and more appreciation for Christian Scripture:

> I needed to find him completely at leisure if I were to pour it all out, and I never did so find him. Nonetheless I listened to him *straightforwardly expounding the word of truth* to the people every Sunday, and as I listened I became more and more convinced that

---

3. *Confessions*, VI.2.2.

it was possible to unravel all those cunning knots of calumny in which the sacred books had been entangled by tricksters who had deceived me and others. I came to realize that your spiritual children, whom you had brought to a new birth by grace from their mother, the Catholic Church, did not in fact understand the truth of your creating human beings in your image in so crude a way that they believed you to be determined by the form of a human body. Although I had not even a faint or shadowy notion of what a spiritual substance could be like, I was filled with joy, albeit a shamefaced joy, at the discovery that what I had barked against for so many years was not the Catholic faith but the figments of carnal imagination.[4]

One of the major obstacles that held Augustine back from accepting, or even being open to, Christian doctrine was the false belief that Christians maintained that God had a physical body, with hands, feet, etc. When Ambrose clearly taught that the Catholic Church did not espouse this doctrine Augustine was overjoyed; it was as if a great weight had been lifted off of his shoulders. For Augustine understood that if God had a physical body, like humans, God would necessarily be limited and hence not God. He could not consider Christianity until he understood that Christianity did not in fact teach such a self-contradictory and absurd proposition. Knowing that Christians saw God as a spiritual being was freeing for Augustine, even though he did not fully understand what it meant to say God was a spiritual being. Another clarification that Augustine received from the preaching of Ambrose was the fact that many Old Testament passages did not have to be understood literally but could in fact be understood figuratively. On this point, Augustine does not tell us of any specific Old Testament passages that Ambrose clarified for him, but only that Ambrose did so and that Augustine was forever grateful to him for that. One can only wonder if the caring and intelligent pastor Ambrose tailored some content in his sermons precisely to teach this new heretic from Rome. Certainly, when Monnica began attending church in Milan regularly during the week for prayer and other activities, Ambrose was aware of her concerns. I am certain that a mother like Monnica would have told Ambrose about Augustine's spiritual condition. Augustine recalls with joy how he often heard Ambrose saying in his sermons, "*The letter is death-dealing, but the spirit gives life*" (*Conf.* VI.4.6). I suggest this was no coincidence, but a wise pastor feeding one of his flock (or potential flock) the spiritual food he needed at the time.

4. Ibid., VI.3.4.

After having a steady diet of Ambrose's preaching, Augustine says he actually "began to prefer Catholic doctrine" (*Conf.* VI.4.6). He even began to get a newfound respect for some of the more difficult doctrines of the church:

> But I came to see that in commanding that certain things must be believed without demonstration the Church was a good deal more moderate and very much less deceitful than those parties who rashly promised knowledge and derided credulity, but then went on to demand belief in a whole host of fabulous and absurd myths which certainly could not be demonstrated.[5]

This comment certainly refers to the Manichaeans. Now that Augustine had left that group and was listening with an open mind and heart to Christian doctrine, he could make an objective assessment of both groups. He concluded that Christian doctrine was far less extreme than he had previously thought and certainly far less extreme than the "absurd myths" of the Manichaeans. Moreover, Augustine was beginning to have an understanding of what it means to have faith. He realizes that there are many things people believe on the testimony of others. For example, on the testimony of others, Augustine points out, we take it for granted that we were born of our particular parents, yet we could not have known this without believing what we heard from others (*Conf.* VI.5.7). In this way, Augustine, who previously needed to prove everything by reason, came to realize that faith in God is reasonable, precisely because people necessarily and reasonably have faith in many things that they simply take for granted. Because of the preaching of Ambrose, Augustine came to realize that truth is not found by reason alone, but in Christian Scripture. Regarding this newfound respect for Scripture, he states:

> Having already heard many parts of the sacred books explained in a reasonable and acceptable way, I came to regard those passages which had previously struck me as absurd, and therefore repelled me, as holy and profound mysteries. The authority of the sacred writings seemed to me all the more deserving of reverence and divine faith in that scripture was easily accessible to every reader, while yet guarding a mysterious dignity in its deeper sense. In plain words and very humble modes of speech it offered itself to

5. Ibid., VI.5.7.

everyone, yet stretched the understanding of those who were *not shallow-minded*.[6]

In reflecting back on this portion of his life, Augustine sees God's guiding hand in all of this: "I was tossed to and fro and you steered me aright. I wandered down the wide road of the world, but you did not desert me" (*Conf.* VI.6.8).

During this time, that is, when Augustine was beginning to have an appreciation for Christian Scripture and the church, he was challenged to examine his life in a more profound way. This came about as a consequence of Augustine's position as teacher of rhetoric. He was scheduled to do a eulogy for an emperor. As he recalls, "I would tell plenty of lies with the object of winning favor with the well-informed by my lying" (*Conf.* VI.6.9). He prepared his speech and headed off to deliver it, but as he was passing through a district in Milan he saw an intoxicated beggar enjoying himself. The contrast between the anxiety building within him regarding the speech he was on his way to deliver and the sight of this joyful beggar challenged Augustine to consider his own life and those of his comrades. In vivid detail, Augustine describes his condition:

> I groaned and pointed out to my friends who were with me how many hardships our idiotic enterprises entailed. Goaded by greed, I was dragging my load of unhappiness along, and feeling it all the heavier for being dragged. Yet while all our efforts were directed to the attainment of unclouded joy, it appeared that this beggar had already beaten us to the goal, a goal which we would perhaps never reach ourselves.[7]

This beggar caused Augustine to consider his life up to this point and how it had not been as successful as he had hoped. For example, for all the work he exerted to become an excellent teacher, when he began his teaching duties in Carthage, he was met with rowdy students whose behavior he despised. In fact, their bad behavior influenced him to leave Carthage for another job in Rome. Yet when he arrived in Rome he was even more disappointed, because many of the students in Rome were dishonest. As a result, when an appointment opened up in Milan for a master teacher of rhetoric, he had to use his influence among the Manichaeans (the group he had secretly rejected but was still living with) to get himself this job. So he

---

6. Ibid., VI.5.8.

7. Ibid., VI.6.9.

came to Milan and met the great Ambrose. Now in Milan, God was using Bishop Ambrose to teach him, and he was making progress. But when he had to do this eulogy, the changes that were taking place in his heart and mind forced him to confront what he was really doing in taking on this assignment. He was not giving a prestigious eulogy for an emperor that he could be proud of; rather he was about to tell a bunch of lies to people he hoped to impress. Consequently, when he saw the beggar being happy, he realized how unhappy he was. The beggar, who had gotten drunk with the few coins he collected honestly from persons passing by, was joyful, while Augustine was miserable. And this particular assignment showed him why he had no joy: he was not going to use his teaching gift to help anyone but rather going to tell a bunch of lies to win the favor of others. This was a moment of truth for Augustine, because he was forced to examine his life in general and his current actions in particular. Augustine would admit, of course, that the happiness of the beggar was not a true happiness or joy either (in reference to God's ideal); but Augustine's own condition was far worse, because the joy he was seeking was even more unreal than that of the beggar. Why? It was more unreal, Augustine insists, because the beggar could go and sleep off his intoxication, while he and his friends had to drag around their misery every day (*Conf.* VI.6.10). This revelation caused Augustine to accept the fact not only that he was unhappy but also that he would never be happy living the way he was currently living. The good life that he had so desperately wanted had eluded him and his friends. Augustine did not want to trade places with the beggar, but the beggar taught him that true happiness was not to be found in the vanity and dishonesty that had characterized his life up to that point. He would come to understand that true happiness is to be found in God alone, but he was yet to discover this.

In the next section (*Conf.* VI.7.12), Augustine discusses his friend Alypius and how God was working in both of their lives, although neither of them knew it at the time. Augustine cites several examples of such working; I will mention two that happened early in his teaching career. In his first example, Augustine recalls how Alypius would not attend his classes regularly because of a prior dispute that he had had with Alypius' father. Nonetheless, Alypius would attend his class from time to time; and, on one of these rare occasions, Augustine just happened to be lecturing on the games, the public entertainments that he calls "Carthaginian immoral amusements." In his lecture, he insisted that these amusements were a waste of time for the serious student. Alypius heard this and took Augustine's lecture as if he was speaking to him personally. This was not Augustine's intention, but looking back on this incident, he now sees God's providence at work:

> You know, our God, that I did not think at the time about cur-
> ing Alypius of this bane. Yet he took my illustration to himself,
> believing that I had used it solely on his account; and what another
> person might have regarded as a reason for being angry with me
> this honest young man regarded rather as a reason to be angry
> with himself and loving more ardently. Long ago you had told
> us, weaving the advice into your scriptures, *Offer correction to a*
> *wise man, and he will love you for it.* Yet I had not corrected him
> myself. You make use of all of us, witting or unwitting, for just
> purposes known to you, and you made my heart and tongue into
> burning coals with which to cauterize a promising mind that was
> wasting away, and heal it.[8]

Alypius was in fact delivered for a time from his addiction to the games, until he was tempted some time later by a group of friends. One day when he and a group of his friends were together, they decided to attend the games that were being held that day. Alypius informed his friends that he had stopped attending those games, but they insisted that he join them. When he refused, they jokingly dragged him along with them. At this, he told his friends that they might take his body there but that his mind would be elsewhere. They carried him along anyway to see if he could make good on his promise. When the games began, Alypius did indeed close his eyes to prevent himself from viewing the action in the arena. However, Alypius underestimated the power of those games and their ability to pull him back into their grip. Once the games began and the crowds began to roar, curios-ity got the better of him. Alypius opened his eyes to see what was happen-ing, and, "as he saw the blood he gulped the brutality along with it; he did not turn away but fixed his gaze there and drank in the frenzy, not aware of what he was doing, reveling in the wicked contest and intoxicated on sanguinary pleasure" (*Conf.* VI.8.13). He was no longer a silent participant but an active spectator likes the rest. From that point on, his friends did not have to drag him to the games; he went willingly. Alypius would eventually break his addiction to the games, but that came much later. Augustine is making a simple point in retelling this story: an individual must not trust in

---

8. Ibid., VI.7.12.

her or his flesh but in the strength of the Lord. This is certainly something we can consider today. No addict needs to tempt him or herself with the very thing that previously enslaved him or her. Moreover, being free today does not mean one is not susceptible to future enslavement. Again, Augustine's lesson here is a good one: put no confidence in the flesh.

Another incident Augustine recounts for us regarding the life of his dear friend Alypius happened years earlier, when Alypius was a student of Augustine in Carthage. While he was innocently walking in the market-place another student had brought an axe which he used to gain access to a silversmith shop. Alypius was not aware of the student's actions, but the owner of the store heard the noise from below and went up to see who was trying to enter his store. At the same time the owner and his assistants came up the stairs to check out the situation, Alypius had innocently picked up the axe that the thief left behind. The owner saw him with the axe in his hand and dragged him off, declaring to the people, "We have caught the thief red-handed" (*Conf.* VI.9.14). Fortunately for Alypius, as he is being taking off for punishment, a certain architect, who had previously seen him at a senator's house, intervened. He took control of the situation, questioning the parties involved until he got to the truth. Upon questioning a slave boy, he got him to confess that it was his master that had committed the crime. Alypius was set free but not without learning a serious lesson. Augustine speaks to the value of this painful lesson.

> You allowed him to be arrested by the temple-guards as a thief; and I think, our God, that you did so for no other reason than to ensure that this youth, who was destined to be such a great man, should learn even at this early stage that in judicial hearing one person ought not to be condemned too easily through the rash gullibility of another.[9]

Thus, when Augustine reflects back on his life, he sees the providence of God not only in his life but in the life of his friends as well. Many of them would eventually follow him into the church, and Alypius, a man of integrity, would become a pastor as well.

Augustine was now thirty years old, and he, along with his African friends Alypius and Nebridius, were facing a crisis: they were finding no pleasure or happiness in the life they were then living. In fact, they were sad a good deal of the time. Augustine recalls this low point:

9. Ibid., VI.9.14.

> So then there were three gaping mouths, three individuals in need, gasping out their hunger to one another and looking to you to give them their food in due time. By your merciful providence our worldly behavior always brought bitter disappointments, but whenever we sought to discern the reason why we should suffer them, we met only darkness. So we went away, moaning, "How long are we to go on like this?" We were perpetually asking this question, but even as we asked it we made no attempt to change our ways, because we had no light to see what we should grasp instead, if we were to let go of them.[10]

At the same time Augustine and his friends are discussing how unhappy there were, Augustine recalls that he is now thirty years of age and rues the time he wasted searching for wisdom and happiness from the age of nineteen. What a waste of time, and yet he would not stop his pursuit of the happy life. He even recalls saying, "Tomorrow I will find it, it will appear plainly, and I will grasp it" (*Conf.* VI.11.18). But this did not happen. As a possible solution to their condition, Augustine and his friends discussed how they could live together in a community and spend all their time seeking wisdom and happiness. The only problem with this proposition, however, was that some of them were married and others of them were soon to be married. Consequently, when they thought about discussing this with their wives and how their wives might take this, their elaborate plan fell apart.

To add to this mounting pressure that Augustine was feeling about his condition, his mother was seeing his progress toward becoming a Christian and pressuring him to take a wife. She even asked God to give her another dream about a marriage for her son. When this did not happen, she did as most mothers do and took matters into her own hands. She found a young girl for her son. Augustine liked the girl, so he consented to marry her. The only problem, however, was that she was not yet of marriageable age, and so he had to wait two years before he could legally marry her. Once he was engaged to be married, his common-law wife was viewed as a hindrance. As a result, they had to separate. She returned to Africa, vowing never to touch another man and leaving the son of their union in his charge. Some scholars have criticized Augustine for this move, pointing out that he does not even mention his common-law wife's name after living with her for over ten and perhaps as many as fourteen years. However, in that culture,

10. Ibid., VI.10.17.

once he had made a commitment to a wife, his new family would have found it unacceptable for him to continue living with his concubine. She had to leave, and for him to refrain from publicizing her name was more a sign of respect than of neglect.[11] This was the common practice of his contemporaries and was even tolerated by the church at the time.[12] Nonetheless, Augustine does speak of the pain this separation caused him. But it appears that the only pain that really concerned Augustine was how much he would suffer in the absence of sexual fulfillment: "I faced two years of waiting before I could marry the girl to whom I was betrothed, and I chafed at the delay, for I was no lover of marriage but the slave of lust. So I got myself another woman" (*Conf.* VI.15.25). On this point, Augustine can be criticized—and clearly criticizes himself—for wanting, at this time in his life, nothing from a woman but sex to fulfill his lust. He was no lover of marriage (he admits) but certainly a slave to his lust. He can certainly be admired also for his honestly.

In closing book VI, Augustine mentions his fear of God's future judgment. Although he was not yet in the church, he had been taught about God's judgment from his youth. And so Augustine, even in his darkest moment, says, "The only thing that restrained me from being sucked still deeper into the whirlpool of carnal lusts was the fear of death and of your judgment, which throughout all the swings of opinion had never been dislodged from my heart" (*Conf.* VI.16.26).

It was precisely because of his belief in God's judgment that he found the arguments of Epicurus, a very popular philosopher (b. 341 BCE), lacking. Thus he posed the following question to his friends: "If we were immortal, and lived in a state of perpetual bodily pleasure without fear of losing it, why should we not be happy?"[13] And "would there be anything else to seek?"[14] The followers of Epicurus taught that the gods neither reward nor punish evil. Thus an Epicurean could live the happy life without any fear of judgment, for the Epicureans believed that death was the end of both body and soul. Augustine did fear the judgment of God and he was

---

11. Clark, *Augustine*, 60.

12. That is, unmarried men were allowed to have common-law wives before they got married, according to the Council of Toledo (400 CE), canon 17.

13. Ibid., VI.16.26. For a discussion on the Epicureans and what they believed, see *Cambridge Dictionary of Philosophy*, s.v. "Epicureanism."

14. *Confessions*, VI.16.26.

not happy, because he believed there was something more than just the misery he and his friends were experiencing. Thus, his quest continued.

DISCUSSION QUESTIONS FOR CHAPTER 6

1. Discuss Augustine's opening prayer. Is there anything that has happened in your life that can help you relate to what he says here?

2. Why is Monnica excited to hear that Augustine is no longer a Manichaean, but not totally surprised? What other responses does she have regarding this good news?

3. Why did Monnica hold Bishop Ambrose in such high regard?

4. Is there anyone in your life who did for you what Ambrose did for Augustine?

5. Why was it important to honor the martyrs in the early church?

6. Discuss Augustine's view of Ambrose as pastor, preacher, and teacher.

7. What were the results of Augustine's listening to Ambrose each Sunday?

8. What did Ambrose mean when he said, *"The letter is death-dealing, but the spirit gives life"*? How was this helpful to Augustine?

9. Why did Augustine eventually say that he began to prefer Catholic doctrine?

10. What happened to Augustine when he saw a beggar on his way to a speaking engagement?

11. Why did Augustine say, "His joy was more unreal than that of the beggar"?

12. Why did Augustine include Alypius in his *Confessions*?

13. Discuss the separation between Augustine and his live-in mistress.

14. Discuss the arrangements of Augustine's new marriage. Discuss his age and the possible age of his future bride.

15. What do you think about Augustine's problem with lust? Was it an addiction or something every young person experiences?

7

Ideas concerning God and the Problem of Evil

IN BOOKS I THROUGH VI Augustine has given the reader a somewhat autobiographical sketch of his life up to this point. In book VII, however,
Augustine does not appear to be interested in continuing an autobiographical sketch of his life. Rather, he uses book VII to discuss in more depth
issues he has raised earlier. The two most pressing concerns are his concept
of God and the problem of evil. Other issues are raised as well, such as
astrology, but his main concern in book VII is telling us how he grew in his
knowledge of God and in his understanding of how to think about God and
how he arrived at his solution to the problem of evil.

Concerning his understanding of God, Augustine narrates again how
he is elated to learn that the Catholic Church does not teach that God has
a physical body like that of humans. From the preaching of Ambrose he
learned that God is a spirit. Although he was excited to know this, Augustine admits that he did not know what it meant to say that God is spirit.
He also admits that he had a hard time getting the idea of a corporeal notion of God out of his imagination. Consequently, even though he did not
believe God had a physical body like humans, he began to imagine God as
being "something corporeal and spread out in space throughout the world"
(*Conf.* VII.1.1). He soon rejected this position, however. If God were spread
out in this way, he reasoned, then larger things would contain larger parts
of God and smaller things smaller parts of God. For example, an elephant
would contain more of God than a sparrow, simply because an elephant is

larger. In this theory, God would be "distributed piecemeal throughout the elements of the world, again with larger things containing larger parts of God and smaller things, smaller parts of God" (*Conf.* VII.1.2). Augustine rejected this as patently absurd.

In section 2.3 of book VII, Augustine discusses another argument concerning God that he had received from his friend Nebridius, saying that he wished he had been aware of it earlier so that he could have presented it to "those self-deceivers," as he now calls the Manichaeans. Here is the argument:

> Those so-called powers of darkness, which they always postulate as a horde deployed in opposition to you: what would they have done to you if you had refused to fight? If the reply is that they could have inflicted some injury on you, it would imply that you are subject to violation and therefore destructible. If, on the other hand, it is denied that they had power to injure you, there would have been no point in fighting.[1]

In view of the concept of God that Augustine had now come to, this argument made perfect sense. Augustine states in section 1.1 of book VII that he now understood that, whatever God is, God must be imperishable, inviolable, and unchangeable. So the first question stated above can now be reworded to say: Since God is imperishable, inviolable, and unchangeable, God cannot be violated in any way; no force could injure God, and therefore there would be no point in God fighting any force that sought to injure him. If, on the other hand, one supposes that some force could injure God, then the entity so injured could not be God according to Augustine's understanding, for God by definition must be imperishable, inviolable, and unchangeable. Augustine goes on to say that the Manichaeans went on to claim that God was involved in such a fierce fight with these evil forces that a part of God's very substance was entangled by these hostile forces. Augustine rejects this as contradicting the nature of God as imperishable, inviolable, and unchangeable, and so he concludes:

> The foregoing argument was therefore quite sufficient, and I ought to have squeezed these people from my gullet and vomited them out, for no escape was left them from the horrible sacrilege of heart and tongue they were committing by thinking and speaking of you in this fashion.[2]

1. *Confessions*, VII.2.3.
2. Ibid.

The "horrible sacrilege" committed by the Manichaeans lay in their assertion that God could be violated by the forces of evil.

Thus, the first step in Augustine's new understanding of God was to accept the scriptural account of God, according to which God is imperishable. This revelation began with the preaching of Bishop Ambrose.

In section 3.4 of book VII, Augustine returns to his discussion of evil before going on with his consideration of the nature of God. Augustine's view of evil is in many ways related to his view of God, for Augustine insists that whatever evil is, it cannot in any way cause defilement or alteration to the unchangeable God (*Conf.* VII.3.4).

Having said that, Augustine begins to explore an explanation of evil that he had heard earlier, namely, that "the cause of evil is the free decision of our will, in consequence of which we act wrongly and suffer your righteous judgment" (*Conf.* VII.3.5). From this premise, Augustine begins his inquiry into the problem of evil. First, Augustine remarks that he was aided in his search by the fact that when he wanted or did not want something, he was absolutely certain that no one else but himself was wanting or not wanting it. Thus, he perceived that the root of his sin lay in his desires. Augustine then asked, "Who made me? Was it not my God, who is not merely good, but Goodness itself?" (*Conf.* VII.3.5) Answering the second question in the affirmative, he concludes that God, must be good. But that conclusion prompts a further question:

> Whence, then, did I derive this ability to will evil and refuse good? Is it in me simply so that I should deserve the punishment I suffer? Who established that ability in me, who planted in me this bitter cutting, when my whole being is from my most sweet God? If the devil is responsible, where did the devil come from? If he was a good angel who was transformed into a devil by his own perverted will, what was the origin of this evil will in him that turned him into a devil, when an angel is made entirely by the supremely good creator?[3]

After pondering these and other questions, Augustine is certain that he must consider evil in light of the truth that a good God created everything good (*Conf.* VII.5.7). As a result, Augustine reasons that "things prone to destruction are good, since this destruction would be out of the question if they were either supremely good or not good at all" (*Conf.* VII.11.17). To understand Augustine's reasoning here, it is important to bear in mind that

3. Ibid., VII.3.5.

to be "supremely good" is to be God and therefore indestructible. Of course nothing is supremely good but God, yet everything else is good because a good God created it. "It follows then," Augustine continues, "that either destruction harms nothing, which is impossible, or that all things which suffer harm are being deprived of some good; this conclusion is beyond cavil" (VII.11.17). Moreover, Augustine reasons, if something were deprived of all its good, it would be nonexistent, for as long as something exists, it must be good because God created it this way. Augustine has thus arrived at the conclusion that evil is the absence or privation of good and believes he has thus solved the problem of evil:

> Everything that exists is good, then; and so evil, the source of which I was seeking, cannot be a substance, because if it were, it would be good. Either it would be an indestructible substance, and that would mean it was very good indeed, or it would be a substance liable to destruction—but then it would not be destructible unless it were good.[4]

For Augustine then, evil is not a substance, because if it were a substance, it would be good, for God created all things good. It follows, then, that the Manichaean view, which asserted that some fundamental evil force exists in opposition to God, is false, because it implies that evil is a substance, that is, that it has some positive existence. Moreover, moral evil, according to Augustine, is rooted in our will: when we chose to do things in opposition to God's plan, we do evil and harm ourselves, but we do not harm God. In fact, Augustine would say in regard to God and evil, "for you evil has no being at all, and this is true not of yourself only but of everything you have created, since apart from you there is nothing that could burst in and disrupt the order you have imposed on it" (*Conf.* VII.13.19). Thus, his understanding of evil is founded on his enlightened view of God, that God must be imperishable, inviolable, and unchangeable. And if the imperishable God created all things good, then everything that is a substance must be good. Since evil is not good, it is therefore not a substance.

In section 10.16 of book VII, Augustine recounts a vision that further deepened his understanding of God:

> Warned by these writings that I must return to myself,[5] I entered under your guidance the innermost places of my being; but only

---

4. Ibid., VII.12.18.

5. Augustine does not tell us here which writings he is referring to. Is he referring

because you had become my helper was I able to do so. I entered, then, and with the vision of my spirit, such as it was, I saw the incommutable light far above my spiritual ken, transcending my mind: not this common light which every carnal eye can see, nor any light of the same order but greater, as though this common light were shinning much more powerfully, far more brightly, and so extensively as to fill the universe. The light I saw was not this common light at all but something different from all these things. Nor was it higher than my mind in the sense that oil floats on water or the sky is above earth; it was exalted because this very light made me, and I was below it because by it I was made. Anyone who knows truth knows it, and whoever knows it knows.eternity. Love knows it.[6]

As Augustine begins to reveal to us what he saw in his vision, it becomes clear that he was allowed to see (if only momentarily) the glorified Christ. For Christ is both the light which Scripture speaks about and the one who made us (John 1:1–4). Moreover, this revelation can only be known through truth and love; and for Augustine God is truth and love. So it is through God's grace that he is allowed this vision. Augustine's discussion of this vision turns into a reason to praise God:

O eternal Truth, true Love, and beloved Eternity, you are my God, and for you I sigh day and night. As I first began to know you, you lifted me up and showed me that while that which I might see exists indeed, I was not yet capable of seeing it. Your rays beamed intensely upon me, beating back my feeble gaze, and I trembled with love and dread. I knew myself to be far away from you in a region of unlikeness, and I seemed to hear your voice from on high: "I am the food of the mature; grow then, and you will eat me. You will not change me into yourself like bodily food: you will be changed into me." And I recognized that you have chastened man for his sin and caused my soul to dwindle away like a spider's web, and I said, "Is truth then a nothing, simply because it is not spread out through space either finite or infinite?" Then from afar you cried to me, "By no means, for *I am who am.*"[7]

to the writings of Plotinus or other Platonists or to Scripture? From what he goes on to describe, I would argue that he is referring to Scripture. For he says that this *light* is not any *light* but the very *light* that made me. In my opinion, this is a reference to Christ, the Eternal Word as described in the prologue to John's gospel (1:1–14).

6. *Confessions*, VII.10.16.

7. Ibid.

The first words that Augustine reports having heard came from a voice from on high saying, "I am the food of the mature; grow then, and you will eat me." This clearly refers to the Christian Eucharist, in which believers partake of the body of Christ and in doing so remember and give thanks for his sacrifice for humankind. The second thing that Augustine heard responded to the question he had posed to the divine: "Is Truth [i.e., God] a nothing, simply because it is not spread out through space either finite or infinite?" This is the question that Augustine had been considering after he realized that God did not have a physical body like humans: "Is God, the eternal truth, spread out in space?" In his vision, Augustine receives a direct response to his question: "By no means, for *I am who am.*" The reference here is to Exodus 3:14, God's revelation of his name (or perhaps more precisely that he is beyond all names) to Moses at the burning bush. The logic here may not be immediately apparent, but one can understand this statement to mean that Augustine is being told to abandon his speculations about God's nature, avoiding any conceptions of God as somehow material (as would be the case if, as Augustine once imagined, God were spread out as a substance in space) and concern himself simply with the reality of God's existence, "that I am who am."

Augustine has this to say concerning the voice he heard: "I heard it as one hears a word in the heart, and no possibility of doubt remained to me; I could more easily have doubted that I was alive than that truth exists, truth that is seen and understood through the things that are made" (*Conf.* VII.10.16). In this vision, the divine gives Augustine not only the answer to his pressing question, but a revelation, if only the merest glimpse, of at least two persons in the godhead. Toward the end of book VII (17.23), Augustine speaks of another vision of the divine. Before doing so, however, he turns to other issues. One such issue is astrology.

In section 6.7 of book VII, Augustine informs his readers how he finally came to be convinced that astrology was a fraud. Augustine had a friend named Firminus whose father was devoted to astrology and who had a friend who was equally devoted to the craft. Because of this devotion, each was careful to cast the horoscopes at the birth of everyone in his household, even of the animals. Now when Firminus' mother was pregnant with him, it happened that a slave girl at the home of his father's friend was also expecting. Both women gave birth simultaneously. Thus, both offspring had exactly the same horoscope, "even in the finest detail, the one to his son and the other to his slave" (*Conf.* VII.6.8). Of course, Firminus, who was brought up in a house of means, received a good education and enjoyed the good life that his status afforded him. The slave child, on the other hand, went on serving his master and receiving the things afforded a person of that class. Thus, Augustine was able to conclude with certainty that the practice of astrology was not based on skill, but luck; one's station in life, especially in the stratified society of the late Roman Empire, had a great influence on one's potential for success or lack thereof, yet in this case astrology passed over this difference completely. Augustine then turns to his knowledge of Scripture to make the same point. In recounting the birth of Esau and Jacob, twin brothers that were born moments apart, Augustine points out that a practitioner of this craft would have to assign the same reading to both of them as well; yet we know from Scripture that their lives were vastly different. From this Augustine concludes, "For in truth it is you, Lord, who are at work, you, the supremely just ruler of the universe, though those who consult astrologers and those who are consulted know it not" (*Conf.* VII.6.10). Here, Augustine offers even today's reader a reasoned justification for rejecting astrology.

Another issue that Augustine here comes to terms with is that of Neoplatonism, a philosophical current that had great influence on him. In section 9.13 of book VII Augustine discusses his reading of some books by Platonists that had been translated from Greek into Latin. Augustine now believes that God wanted to show him through this reading how the prideful are thwarted by God while the humble receive mercy. As he reflects on these books, he points out several times that the gospel message concerning Christ was not found in them:

> I did not read in them that your only-begotten Son, coeternal with you, abides before all ages and above all ages, and that of *his fullness* our souls receive, to become blessed thereby, and that by participation in that Wisdom which abides in itself they are made new in order to become wise; but that *at that time of our weakness he died for the wicked*, and that you did not spare even your only Son, but delivered him up for us all, these things are not to be found there. For you have *hidden these matters from the sagacious and shrewd, and revealed them to little ones*, so that those who toil under heavy burdens may come to him and he may give them relief, because he is gentle and humble in heart.[8]

---

8. Ibid., VII.9.14.

Augustine now understands how God thwarts the proud, because he was that proud person who sought vain things in the writings of the Platonists. Their works, however great, did not have the truth concerning Jesus; therefore, they did not have truth as Augustine would later come to understand and appreciate it. Nonetheless, Augustine believes his exposure to the writings of the Platonists was part of God's plan for his life:

> I believe that you willed me to stumble upon them before I gave my mind to your scriptures, so that the memory of how I had been affected by them might be impressed upon me when later I had been brought to a new gentleness through the study of your books, and your fingers were tending my wounds; thus insight would be mine to recognize the difference between presumption and confession, between those who see the goal but not the way to it and the Way to our beatific homeland, a homeland to be not merely described but lived in.[9]

Even though the writings of the Platonists did not help Augustine find Jesus, they were of some benefit to him in grasping the divine and thus continued to influence the direction of his thought:

> But in those days, after reading the books of the Platonists and following their advice to seek for truth beyond corporeal forms, I turned my gaze toward your invisible reality, trying to understand it through created things, and though I was rebuffed I did perceive what that reality was which the darkness of my soul would not permit me to contemplate.[10]

With this in mind, we can turn to the last section of Augustine's second vision as recorded in book VII, where he says this of his ability to reason or understand:

> It strove to discover what this light was that bedewed it when it cried out unhesitatingly that the Unchangeable is better than anything liable to change; it sought the fount whence flowed its concept of the Unchangeable—for unless it had in some fashion recognized Immutability, it could never with such certainty have judged it superior to things that change. And then my mind attained to *That Which Is*, in the flash of one tremulous glance. Then indeed did I perceive your invisible reality through created things, but to keep my gaze there was beyond my strength. I was forced

9. Ibid., VII.20.26.
10. Ibid.

back through weakness and returned to my familiar surround-
ings, bearing with me only a loving memory, one that yearned for
something of which I had caught the fragrance, but could not yet
feast upon.[11]

Again, Augustine was allowed to gaze upon the divine, but only for a
moment; he had been allowed to catch "the fragrance" of God, but nothing
more.

These visions apparently whetted Augustine's thirst for a deeper experience of the divine, for he says that he now began to look for a way to find
the strength to enjoy God (*Conf.* VII.18.25). Of course, after he was saved
and thoroughly immersed in Scripture that relationship would come; but
did he in fact have such profound, if fleeting, revelations of God before he
was saved? As stated in the opening, Augustine is not interested in giving
us an exact timeline for the events he is describing. It appears that his main
point here is simply to share these thoughts and visions to show his readers—even those who have not yet embraced Christ—what is possible to
those who genuinely seek God—and to set the stage for the transformation
he will depict in the next book.

11. Ibid., VII.17.23.

DISCUSSION QUESTIONS FOR CHAPTER 7

1. How is book VII different from the first six books of the *Confessions*?

2. What are the two main issues Augustine is concerned with in book VII?

3. After Augustine is happy to find that the church did not believe God had a physical body, like humans, what was the next problem he faced?

4. Discuss Augustine's early view of God as being spread out throughout the universe. Why does he reject this view of God?

5. What was the argument that his friend Nebridius gave him and what is his point concerning it?

6. What are the three attributes of God that Augustine mentions at the beginning of book VII that are crucial in helping him understand God?

7. How does Augustine's understanding of God affect his understanding of evil?

8. What conclusions did Augustine finally arrive at regarding the problem of evil and how did he arrive at this conclusion? Do you agree or disagree?

9. How does Augustine's new understanding of God and evil give him fuel to combat the teaching of the Manichaeans?

10. What are your thoughts concerning Augustine's first vision?

11. What finally convinced Augustine that astrology was a fraud?

12. Discuss Augustine's assessment of the Platonist books he read.

13. How did the Platonist writings help Augustine seek the divine?

14. Why does Augustine say it was good for him to have read them first, even before reading Scripture?

15. What do you think of Augustine's second vision?

8

St. Antony / Conversion

IN BOOK VIII OF Augustine's *Confessions*, Augustine describes his final struggles on his way to being converted to Christianity. The tensions that he has been describing in books I through VII are finally resolved at the end of book VIII. As a result, it is only fitting that he begins this book with praise and thanksgiving:

> In a spirit of thankfulness let me recall the mercies you lavished on me, O my God; to you let me confess them. May I be flooded with love for you until my very bones cry out, "Who is like you, O Lord?" Let me offer you a sacrifice of praise, for you have snapped my bonds. How you have broken them I will relate, so that all your worshipers who hear my tale may exclaim, "Blessed be the Lord, blessed in heaven and on earth, for great and wonderful is his name."[1]

Again we must not forget the evangelistic aspect of Augustine's *Confessions*, as stated here. Augustine is careful to mention that he wants to relate how he was converted (how God broke him) so that all who worship God and those that do not yet worship God may read his account and one day say as he did, "Blessed be the Lord, blessed in heaven and earth, for great and wonderful is his name."

At this pivotal point in Augustine's life, he was attending church regularly and studying Scripture intensely, while losing his ambition for worldly success. He says, "Your words were now firmly implanted in my heart of

---

1. *Confessions*, VIII.1.1.

hearts and I was besieged by you on every side" (*Conf.* VIII.1.1). Augustine was getting closer, yet he still had many questions that were troubling his inquisitive mind. In what he again believes is the providence of God, he was led to meet with Simplicianus, an elderly Christian who had served the Lord since his youth. Not only was Simplicianus a well-respected believer among the Christians who knew him, but he also had the distinction of being the one who stood with Bishop Ambrose at his baptism, acting as his spiritual father. Thus, Bishop Ambrose, the one Augustine held in such high esteem, viewed this man Simplicianus as a father. So with great anticipation Augustine wanted to meet and discuss with Simplicianus some of the issues troubling him. When he finally met Simplicianus, he told him that he had read some of the Platonist writings that were translated into Latin by Victorinus. Simplicianus spoke well of the Platonists, saying that their writings "conveyed in every possible way, albeit indirectly, the truth of God and his Word" (*Conf.* VIII.2.3). This is interesting indeed, for Augustine's assessment of the philosophers was probably favorable at that time. He would later have a different view, which has already been described in book VII. There, Augustine criticizes the writings of the Platonists on the grounds that they did not have (in his view) the truth concerning Jesus, the eternal Word and only begotten Son, in their writings (*Conf.* VII.9.13–15). At the time he met Simplicianus, however, he did not hold this critical position regarding the Platonists. Nor, apparently, did Simplicianus, for in contrast to his qualified endorsement of Platonist philosophy he condemned the writings of the non-Platonist philosophers, saying they were full of fallacies and dishonesty (*Conf.* VIII.2.3). As they continued their conversation, Simplicianus helped Augustine to take another step closer to Christ by relating how the conversion of Victorinus came about. In some ways, Victorinus was the successful person that Augustine was striving to become. He had successfully taught rhetoric in Rome, was well studied in the liberal arts, and had become well respected by those in high society. Yet Victorinus began studying the Christians Scriptures seriously and came to believe that what he read was indeed the truth. As a result, he told Simplicianus one day that he had become a Christian, to which Simplicianus replied, "I will not believe that, nor count you among Christians, until I see you in Christ's Church" (*Conf.* VIII.2.4). Victorinus responded by saying something to the effect that "if this is true, then it's the walls that make one a Christian." His point was a good one, but in Victorinus' case, there was another reason for this comment. Simplicianus relates to Augustine that the real reason for

Victorinus' hesitation in attending church was his fear of criticism from his nonbelieving friends. Nonetheless, as he kept reading Scripture, it dawned upon him that if he continued to be afraid to confess Christ before men, then perhaps Christ would reject him before God and his holy angels, as stated in Scripture (Mark 8:38). Shortly after this revelation, Victorinus told Simplicianus, "Let us go to church: I want to become a Christian" (*Conf.* VIII.2.4). Simplicianus went to church with him, overjoyed at his decision. Shortly after Victorinus' profession of faith, he put his name in for baptism. This was a good decision, but it presented him with yet another challenge. The custom at the time was that anyone approaching baptism would recite (from memory) the baptismal creed before the community of believers. Because Victorinus was a well-known person, the local priest offered him a way to make his confession in a less public way to alleviate any pressure he might feel. This option was also offered to believers that were shy. Victorinus, however, refused this option, recalling how he had taught secular things in public, so why not confess openly the creed of his new faith? Thus, he prepared himself, and on the day of his announcement the following happened:

> As he climbed up to repeat the Creed they all shouted his name to one another in a clamorous outburst of thanksgiving—everyone who knew him, that is; and was there anyone present who did not? Then in more subdued tones the word passed from joyful mouth to joyful mouth among them all: "Victorinus, Victorinus!" Spontaneous was their shout of delight as they saw him, and spontaneous their attentive silence to hear him. With magnificent confidence he proclaimed the true faith, and all the people longed to clasp him tenderly to their hearts. And so they did, by loving him and rejoicing with him, for those affections were like clasping hands.[2]

To the surprise of Victorinus and the religious leaders, there was nothing to fear regarding his decision to become a Christian. Victorinus had built up so much good will among the citizens of Rome (Christian and non-Christian alike) that everyone rejoiced at his decision. Today we can learn from this story as well. If we are not careful, we will become fretful over negative things we imagine might happen. But, like Victorinus, we should make our stand with God and let the rest take care of itself; for often what we imagine is never realized. For Augustine, however, this must have been a powerful story for him to hear at this point in his life. Augustine

2. Ibid., VIII.2.5.

was moving toward God, in that he was reading Scripture and attending church, but he was still wrestling with how to break free from the things of the world and become a Christian. In recounting the wonderful reception Victorinus received at his baptism,[3] the wise Simplicianus gave Augustine the advice he needed by using someone like himself as an example. His example had the desired effect, for Augustine says that after hearing the story of Victorinus he was motived to imitate him (*Conf.* VIII.5.10). In closing out his meeting with Augustine, Simplicianus had one more story about Victorinus he needed to recount. He related to Augustine that during the time of Emperor Julian (361–62 CE), who attempted a restoration of paganism, it was decreed that Christians not be allowed to teach. Victorinus did not complain at this decree but complied, choosing rather to abandon his profession for a period than abandon God's word. Augustine was elated by the life of Victorinus as related to him by Simplicianus, and from this account he was armed with an example of how a person like himself could come to the Lord.

Before continuing his salvation narrative, however, Augustine is provoked to think about the great joy displayed at the announcement of Victorinus' conversion. He compares this to the lack of such joy when less famous persons come to Christ. Why is this so, Augustine asks? Certainly, it is not because the rich are more welcome than the poor in God's kingdom. Augustine knows this is not the case, because Scripture teaches us that God has chosen the weak of the world to shame the strong (1 Cor 1:27–28; Rom 4:17). But as he continues his inquiry, Augustine arrives at a reasonable answer:

> The higher, then, the value set on the soul of Victorinus, which the devil had captured as an impregnable stronghold, and on Victorinus' tongue, which the devil had wielded like a huge, sharp weapon to destroy many, the greater was the gladness with which your children rightly rejoiced on seeing the powerful foe bound by our King and his weaponry seized, cleaned, and made fit to serve in your honor as equipment useful to the Master for every good purpose.[4]

Yes, it is reasonable for persons to be overjoyed when a person comes to the Lord who had been such a force in the world that his or her new

---

3. Baptismal candidates were required to make a statement prior to their baptism. Their baptism could have happened on the day of their confession or a few days later.

4. Ibid., VIII.4.9.

commitment is met initially with surprise and then with great joy. Part of this exuberance stems from having such a powerful and dynamic figure now working for the kingdom of God.

As Augustine pondered the life of Victorinus, he was led to examine his own life, but this time in light of the Scriptures he was studying. As a result, he could clearly see how Galatians 5:7—"You were running well; who prevented you from obeying the truth?"—represents his current condition. That is, the fleshly part of him was at war with the new nature that was trying to break free. Concerning his condition, Augustine says, "The two wills fought it out—the old and the new, the one carnal, the other spiritual—and in their struggle tore my soul apart" (*Conf.* VIII.5.11). Augustine's road to salvation lay through profound and tumultuous inner struggle as he fought to combat his bad habits, using the new teaching he was reading in Scripture. He compares his condition with that of one who is trying to awake himself from a deep sleep but cannot do so. Moreover, in an insightful way, Augustine also relates his sinful condition to the powerful force of habit produced by his continual sinning:

> For the law of sin is that brute force of habit whereby the mind is dragged along and held fast against its will, and deservedly so because it slipped into the habit willingly. In my wretched state, who was there to free me from this death-doomed body, save your grace through Jesus Christ our Lord?[5]

The last line is telling, for Augustine realized that only the grace of God through Jesus Christ could free him from his sinful condition. Thus he knows the way but is not yet able to get to his destination.

Sometime after his conversation with Simplicianus, another Christian, named Ponticianus, came to visit one of his roommates. Augustine is careful to point out that Ponticianus was a fellow African like Alypius, Nebridius, and himself and that thus "he was our compatriot" (*Conf.* VIII.6.14). It appears that Augustine and a few of his elite African friends lived together as they moved about the Roman Empire seeking employment. At the time, Augustine was a teacher of rhetoric in Milan, Alypius an assessor and lawyer, and Nebridius an assistant teacher to Verecundus, a schoolmaster. Ponticianus, their compatriot, held an important post at court. Augustine does not tell us why Ponticianus came to visit them; perhaps he was aware of Augustine's dilemma. In any event, when Ponticianus entered their home,

---

5. Ibid., VIII.5.12.

79

he observed some Scripture (perhaps the letters of Paul) on the table. He then congratulated Augustine, believing that he was a Christian like himself. Augustine informed him that he was not yet a Christian, but simply a student of Scripture. At this announcement, Ponticianus began to witness to his fellow Africans about the gospel by telling them of another African, an Egyptian named St. Antony.

St. Antony, a fourth-century monk and hermit, was one of the most famous of those now known as the Desert Fathers. Many man, and some women, during this period of church history sold their possessions and went out into the desert to fight the demons they found there and to pray for a sinful world. They were also known for working miracles and giving godly advice to those who sought them out. Antony's story comes to us from the great bishop Athanasius, who got to know Antony during his many exiles from his post as bishop of Alexandria in Egypt. He wrote a book entitled *The Life of Antony* so that the hermit's deeds would not be lost to the church. In his book, Athanasius recounts how Antony came to serve the Lord. It just so happened that as Antony attended church one day, he heard the preacher repeat the words of Jesus in his sermon, "*If you want to be perfect, sell all you have and give it to the poor and then come and follow me and you will have riches in heaven*" (Matt 19:21).[6] When Antony heard these words, he took them as if the Lord was speaking to him personally. Shortly afterward, he sold his family's inheritance, saving a small amount for the care of his sister, and then went into the desert to serve the Lord.[7] However, because of his gifts, Antony soon became famous, and other monks (as well as other believers) began seeking him out for advice. As a result, he kept going farther and farther into the desert to avoid the attention, but he was never completely successful. Antony lived to be 105 years of age, and many miracles were attributed to him. Because of his reputation and the book Athanasius wrote about him, many Christians continued to hold Antony in high esteem long after his death. During Augustine's time, more and more holy men and women begin to gather in communities (monasteries), where they could be under the direction of the church and of a spiritual leader. As Ponticianus related the story of Antony, he also informed Augustine that there was a monastery right outside the city of

6. Athanasius, *Antony*, 31.

7. Some of the Christians in the early church went into the desert to fight demons in imitation of Jesus. After Jesus' baptism, Mark records the following: "At once the Spirit sent him out into the desert, and he was in the desert forty days, being tempted by Satan. He was with the wild animals, and angels attended him" (Mark 1:12–13).

Milan, where Bishop Ambrose was the overseer. This information surprised Augustine. When Augustine and his housemates told Ponticianus that they had never heard of Antony or of the community outside of Milan, Ponticianus took this as his cue to go deeper into the life of Antony, to which Augustine says, "Ponticianus went on talking and developing the theme, while we listened, spellbound" (*Conf.* VIII.6.15). Ponticianus continued his testimony concerning Antony, but from a different angle. He recounted to Augustine and his roommates a life-changing incident involving two of his friends at court. One day three of his friends went for a walk along the walls of the court. A short distance into their walk, they divided into two groups, one person walking with Ponticianus and another pair walking together by themselves. The latter pair happened upon a cottage where holy men were living and serving God. As they entered the residence they saw *The Life of Anthony* lying on the table. One of the pair begin to read the book and the following happened:

> His admiration and enthusiasm were aroused, and as he read he began to mull over the possibility of appropriating the same kind of life for himself, by renouncing his secular career to serve you alone. (He belonged to the ranks of so-called administrative officers.) Then quite suddenly he was filled with a love of holiness and a realistic sense of shame and disgust with himself; he turned his gaze toward his friend and demanded, "Tell me: where do we hope all our efforts are going to get us? What are we looking for? In whose cause are we striving? Does life at court promise us anything better than promotion to being Friends of the Emperor? And once we are, will that not be a precarious position fraught with perils? Will it not mean negotiating many a hazard, only to end in greater danger still? And how long would it take us to get there? Whereas I can become a friend of God here and now if I want to."[8]

The young man began to read more from the book of Antony's life and then decided to follow the hermit. He announced to his friend, "I am going to set about it this very moment and in this place. If you have no stomach to imitate me, at least don't stand in my way" (*Conf.* VIII.6.15). To his delight, his friend decided to join him. While all of this was happening, Ponticianus was walking in another part of the garden with his friend. Meeting up with the other two, they were informed of their two friends' decision and how it had come about. Ponticianus and his companion offered their friends

8. *Confessions*, VIII.6.15.

congratulations, cried with them, and then left them behind to fulfill their new calling in the church. Both of these men were engaged to be married when they made their decision to live out a celibate vocation. Yet when their future wives found out, they did not complain, but imitated them by also becoming virgins for the church.[9]

After hearing Ponticianus' story of St. Antony and the two men who embraced the celibate life after reading the life of St. Antony, Augustine was forced to examine his life yet again. And again, he was disgusted with what he found. He began to reflect on the many years he had wasted chasing the wisdom of this world, and he was also led to reflect on his past desire to tame his lust by praying for the gift of chastity. He forced himself to be honest about his previous attitude: "As I prayed to you for the gift of chastity I had even pleaded, 'Grant me chastity and self-control, but please not yet,' I was afraid that you might hear me immediately and heal me forthwith of the morbid lust which I was more anxious to satisfy than to snuff out" (*Conf.* VIII.7.17). That was then, but after hearing of the account of St. Antony and the men who had followed him into the celibate life, his interest in pursuing chastity was renewed afresh. Ponticianus also convinced Augustine of the truth of the gospel. As a result, Augustine reports that his conscience was gnawing away at him with these words: "You have been professing yourself reluctant to throw off your load of illusion because truth was uncertain. Well, it is certain now, yet the burden still weighs you down while other people are given wings on freer shoulders, people who have not worn themselves out with research, nor spent a decade and more reflecting on these questions" (*Conf.* VIII.7.18). When Ponticianus left the house, Augustine was left to his thoughts and the inner turmoil that had been building inside of him. He recalls this inner struggle:

> Within the house of my spirit the violent conflict raged on, the quarrel with my soul that I had so powerfully provoked in our secret dwelling, my heart, and at the height of it I rushed to Alypius with my mental anguish plain on my face. "What is happening to us?" I exclaimed. "What does this mean? What did you make of it? The untaught are rising up and taking heaven by storm, while we with all our dreary teachings are still groveling in this world of flesh and blood! Are we ashamed to follow, just because they

---

9. It is important to note that at this period in the life of the church, many took Paul's admonition to heart that it is better to be single so you can serve the Lord freely than to be married (1 Cor 7:8).

have taken the lead, yet not ashamed of lacking the courage even to follow?"[10]

After speaking these words, Augustine entered the garden next to their house so that he could gather his thoughts. Again, he was assailed with inner turmoil; he was ready to accept Christ, but unable to quell the tumult within himself. He calls this condition a partial willing and partial non-willing that resulted in sickness. And sick he was, as he sat in the garden with his mind racing. Yet as he continued in this condition, Augustine received a revelation about the question that had been troubling him. He recalls:

> The taunts had begun to sound much less persuasive, however; for a revelation was coming to me from that country toward which I was facing, but into which I trembled to cross. There I beheld the chaste, dignified figure of Continence. Calm and cheerful was her manner, though modest, pure and honorable her charm as she coaxed me to come and hesitate no longer, stretching kindly hands to welcome and embrace me, hands filled with a wealth of heartening examples. A multitude of boys and girls were there, a great concourse of youth and persons of every age, venerable widows and women grown old in their virginity, and in all of them I saw that this same Continence was by no means sterile, but the fruitful mother of children conceived in joy from you, her Bridegroom. She was smiling at me, but with a challenging smile, as though to say, "Can you not do what these men have done, these women? Could any of them achieve it by their own strength, without the Lord their God? He it was, the Lord their God, who granted me to them. Why try to stand by yourself, only to lose your footing? Cast yourself on him and do not be afraid: he will not step back and let you fall. Cast yourself upon him trustfully; he will support and heal you."[11]

All of Augustine's props were being knocked out from under him. He had been given sound advice from Simplicianus on how Victorinus (someone like himself) was saved. He then received instructions from a fellow African, Ponticianus, who spoke to him about the gospel and the great St. Antony. After all this, he tells us, his doubts about what he believed to be the truth were gone. But his fear that he would not be able to lead the life of chastity that he so admired still held him back. And now, as he was going

10. *Confessions*, VIII.8.19.

11. Ibid., VIII.11.27.

back and forth in his mind, he was given a revelation (perhaps an open vision) about the gift of chastity: that chastity was not sterile but the fruitful mother of many children conceived in joy from her bridegroom, Christ, and that it was a gift that Augustine was challenged to accept by faith. If he does, he is assured that God "will not step back and let you fall" (*Conf.* VIII.11.27), for God will not only heal him of his sins, but support him in his walk of continence. As a result of this revelation, Augustine is brought to tears:

> I flung myself down somehow under a fig-tree and gave free rein to the tears that burst from my eyes like rivers, as an acceptable sacrifice to you. Many things I had to say to you, and the gist of them, though not the precise words, was: "O Lord, how long? How long? Will you be angry for ever? Do not remember our age-old sins." For by these I was conscious of being held prisoner, I uttered cries of misery: "Why not put an end to my depravity this very hour?"[12]

As Augustine was weeping and speaking to himself in this manner, he heard a child's voice saying to him, "Pick it up and read, pick it up and read" (*Conf.* VIII.12.29). As he pondered the meaning of this, he realized that it was a divine command for him to pick up the Scriptures and read from them. The story of St. Antony, which he had just heard from Ponticianus, came to his mind: Antony, on hearing the gospel text bidding Jesus' followers to sell all they had, give it to the poor, and come follow him, immediately set about putting these words into action. Inspired by Antony and the voice he had heard in the garden, Augustine also moved into action:

> Stung into action, I returned to the place where Alypius was sitting, for on leaving it I had put down there the book of the apostle's letters. I snatched it up, opened it and read in silence the passage on which my eyes first lighted: *Not in dissipation and drunkenness, nor in debauchery and lewdness, nor in arguing and jealousy; but put on the Lord Jesus Christ, and make no provision for the flesh or the gratification of your desires.*[13]

After reading just two verses from Paul's epistle to the Romans (13:13–14), Augustine's suffering and anxiety came to an end, for he declares: "The light of certainty flooded my heart and all dark shades of doubt fled away" (*Conf.* VIII.12.29). Augustine returned and told Alypius how he had been

12. Ibid., VIII.12.28.

13. Ibid., VIII.12.29.

changed and how it had come about. Alypius also informed Augustine of the changes that were taking place in his heart and then asked Augustine what passage he had read. Augustine found the passage, and Alypius read the very next passage for himself: *Make room for the person who is weak in faith* (Rom 14:1) He took that to relate to himself and Augustine, and he too followed his friend into the kingdom of God. After that, they both went inside and told Monnica, who was overjoyed that her prayers were finally answered. Augustine recalls this moment in vivid detail:

> Many years earlier you had shown her a vision of me standing on the rule of faith; and now indeed I stood there, no longer seeking a wife or entertaining any worldly hope, for you had converted me to yourself. In so doing you had also converted her grief into a joy far more abundant than she had desired, and much more tender and chaste than she could ever have looked to find in grandchildren from my flesh.[14]

Augustine's struggles were over; he was saved. By his own admission, his questions had been answered so completely that there was no more doubt about where truth could be found. The truth he was seeking was found in Scripture, which he formerly had criticized. Moreover, his struggles with the flesh had been dwelt with, for he had accepted the challenge to live a life of continence for the Lord. Thus, he can truly say that his mother's joy was more than she desired, for he had begun and would continue as a dedicated servant of God.

14. Ibid., VIII.12.30.

DISCUSSION QUESTIONS FOR CHAPTER 8

1. Discuss Augustine's opening prayer to God. How is this prayer evangelistic?

2. Why was Simplicianus the perfect person to speak with Augustine?

3. What did Simplicianus say about the Platonist philosophers? What did he say about the non-Platonists?

4. Why did Simplicianus say "he would not count Victorinus as a Christian until he came to Church?" Do you agree with this or disagree?

5. Why was the story of how Victorinus got saved important for Augustine to hear at that time in his life?

6. What happened on the day Victorinus had to recite the baptismal creed before the crowd?

7. Why is Augustine concerned with the excessive joy people expressed at the salvation of Victorinus? How does he resolve this?

8. What happened when Ponticianus came to visit one of Augustine's roommates?

9. Why did Augustine say that Ponticianus was our compatriot, referring to him and his roommates?

10. What was the reaction of Augustine and his roommates after hearing the story of St. Antony being recounted to them by Ponticianus?

11. Who was St. Antony and why was he an important figure to many Christians during his lifetime and after his death?

12. What happened to Ponticianus' friends when they went for a walk along the walls of the court? How do you think this affected Augustine who was struggling with lust?

13. Discuss Augustine's revelation or vision that he had regarding continence. What can we learn from this revelation that can help us today?

14. What happened to Augustine under the fig tree?

15. What verses did Augustine read and what was the meaning of this Scripture?

16. Why did this Scripture seem to cut to the heart of Augustine's problems?

9

Baptism and Death

AUGUSTINE OPENS BOOK IX of his *Confessions* with a declaration of praise for what he has come to know. He now knows not only who God is but also who God is in relationship to himself:

> O Lord, I am your servant, I am your servant and your handmaid's son. You burst my bonds asunder, and to you will I offer a sacrifice of praise. May my heart and tongue give praise to you, and all my bones cry out their question, "Who is like you, O Lord?" Yes, let them ask, and then do you respond and say to my soul, "I am your salvation."[1]

After many years of searching for wisdom and the happy life and pursuing worldly fame and fortune, Augustine has surrendered all so that he can declare he is a servant of God. And instead of seeking the wealth of this world, he now declares that God is his wealth, his glory, and his salvation (*Conf.* IX.1.1). But after this wonderful declaration, Augustine asks a question that seems rather odd to this reader: "But where had my power of free decision been throughout those long, weary years, and from what depth, what hidden profundity, was it called forth in a moment, enabling me to bow my neck to your benign yoke and my shoulders to your light burden, O Christ Jesus, my helper and redeemer?" (*Conf.* IX.1.1).

I find this question odd because Augustine has described in great detail throughout books I through VIII how his free will was allowed free rein. When he was a sinful youth stealing pears, his free will was running

1. *Confessions*, IX.1.1.

rampant; it was not hidden. When he was a young adolescent, his free will was pursuing its lustful desires against his mother's wishes. And when Augustine rejected the Scriptures initially, because he found them crude and unsophisticated, his free will made that decision also. When he chose to join the Manichaeans, his free will was likewise at work. So how to answer Augustine's question as to how his free will was brought forth in an instant? I suggest that his free will was not brought forth in an instant. Augustine's free will was there all the time working its desires. But I suggest that God was also working his divine will alongside Augustine's will to bring about the final outcome. If we view human free will in this way, surely we can also ask, as Augustine did, "Who is like you, O Lord?" And the answer for the believer is: *no one.* In our own lives, perhaps, we can look back and see where God's handiwork was guiding us, though we did not perceive this guidance at the time. The mystery remains, however, when we try to understand how we freely reject Christ one day and then freely accept him the next. Certainly, part of this answer can be found in the challenges God allows us to experience so that we might come to see a new point of view. God certainly worked this way with Augustine, bringing him step by step to the point where his mind was ready to accept Christ. He says as much at the end of section 1 of book IX: "My mind was free at last from the gnawing need to seek advancement and riches, to welter in filth and scratch my itching lust" (*Conf.* IX.1.1).

Augustine's thinking had changed, and therefore his free will (or desires) would move in other directions. Augustine's desire to quit his lifelong passion of teaching rhetoric to secular students marked one such change. After his conversion, Augustine desired only to await baptism and serve the Lord in holy continence. Yet he did not know how to go about quitting his job without bringing unwanted attention to himself. As life would have it, while he was considering the appropriate course to take, Augustine became so seriously ill that he could hardly breathe and certainly could not teach. About this opportune illness, Augustine says, "I began to rejoice that a genuine excuse lay to hand which I could use to appease parents who for their children's sake were unwilling even to allow me freedom" (*Conf.* IX.2.4). Because of this illness, Augustine was allowed a respite before he resigned at the end of the holiday break. In the interim, he was allowed to stay on Verecundus' estate, while he and his circle of friends studied Scripture in preparation for their baptism.

Augustine's time of leisure was soon met with grief, however, as two of his friends died unexpectedly. Verecundus, who was very dear to Augustine because he allowed him and his friends to live on his estate while they were awaiting baptism, was the first to pass. When Augustine left his estate in Cassiciacum for a brief period to go to Rome for business, Verecundus died. Augustine was unaware of his death until he returned but found comfort in knowing that Verecundus had become a Christian before his passing. The second friend to succumb was Nebridius. Shortly after their baptism, Nebridius, who had briefly fallen into the error of the gnostic heresy, had corrected his mistake and was doing great work in his homeland. Augustine recalls that "when he was serving you in perfect chastity and continence among his own people in Africa, when his whole household had become Christian through his example, you released him from the flesh. And now he lives in Abraham's bosom" (*Conf.* IX.3.6). So, some time before and immediately after his Christian baptism, Augustine experienced the death of two of his close friends. During this time of suffering, Augustine informs us, he sought relief from the Psalms. "How loudly I cried out to you, my God, as I read the psalms of David, songs full of faith, outbursts of devotion with no room in them for the breath of pride" (*Conf.* IX.6.8). It is important to note here that at this point in his life, when two of his friends and later two of his family members were to die, Augustine fell in love with the Psalms as a way both to deal with his pain and to give God praise. Augustine would go on to write a complete exposition of the psalms that would take him over thirty years to complete. Thus, out of forty years of full-time ministry, thirty were spent writing his commentary on the Psalms (though he wrote much else besides). Much else in Augustine's life shows his devotion to the Psalms. He preached many sermons on them and loved to hear them sung in church. At the death of Augustine's mother, his friend Evodius took up the Psalter and began to sing a psalm. Throughout the pages of the *Confessions* themselves, Augustine constantly quotes or alludes to the Psalms. Finally, on Augustine's deathbed, as the town of Hippo was being seized, he had the short penitential psalms written on the walls of his bedroom so he could read them as he confessed his sins to God.[2] As a person who accused himself of being prideful before his conversion, he read the Psalms until the very end of his life, to prevent this vice from rearing its ugly head (*Conf.* IX.4.8).

---

2. Paulinus, the biographer of Augustine, informs us of this.

In section 11.12 of book IX, Augustine recalls in vivid detail another incident from this period. One day he suffered a terrible toothache, so severe that he could not even speak. It occurred to him that he should request that everyone in the house pray to God for his healing. He wrote this on a piece of paper and passed it to one of his comrades in the house. As they knelt to pray, he was immediately healed of the pain. To this, Augustine says that he was terrified, because he had never experienced anything like this before. However, being the inquisitive person that he was, Augustine had to ask God the following questions: "What was the pain? Where did it go? Augustine could not answer these questions, of course, but he came to believe that this miracle was a sign of God's powerful will[3] and perhaps a testimony that God was with him in a special way before his baptism and would continue to be with him as he prepared to serve God full-time.

When the time for his baptism arrived, Augustine and his friends left the countryside and returned to Milan to be baptized by Bishop Ambrose. On this occasion, his friend Alypius, who would also become an outstanding leader in the church in Africa, joined him, as well as Adeodatus, his son by his departed mistress. Instead of going into details about his experience of baptism, Augustine takes this occasion to speak about the talents of his only son who joined him in being baptized. This is the only place in his writings where he speaks with such passion regarding his son. As a proud father, he writes:

> Very fair had you fashioned him. He was then about fifteen, but surpassed many educated men of weighty learning. I am acknowledging that these were your gifts, O Lord, my God, creator of all things, who are more than powerful enough to give fair form to our deformities, for nothing did I contribute to that boy's making except my fault. It was you, and you alone, who had inspired us to instruct him in your truth as he grew up, and so it is your own gifts that I acknowledge to you. There is a book of ours entitled *The Teacher*, in which he converses with me. You know that all the thoughts there attributed to my interlocutor were truly his, although he was only sixteen years old. Many other things even more wonderful did I observe in him. The brilliance he evinced filled me with awe, for who else but you could be the artificer of such prodigies?[4]

3. *Confessions*, IX.4.12.
4. Ibid., IX.6.14.

Just as Augustine's parents had witnessed the intellectual potential of their son and did everything they could to encourage him, Augustine took every opportunity to encourage and acknowledge the talents of his son, Adeodatus. Moreover, he must have felt great pride and enjoyment to watch his son interact with his friends in lively discussions and then to coauthor a book with him and to study Scripture together in preparation for their baptism. Yet Adeodatus' talents would not be fully realized, because he too was taken away from this life at the tender age of seventeen. Augustine takes pride in describing his many talents but falls silent regarding any details about his death. He does, however, tell us that he was pleased with the short life his son did enjoy. "Very soon you took him away from this life on earth, but I remember him without anxiety, for I have no fear about anything in his boyhood or adolescence; indeed I fear nothing whatever for that man" (*Conf.* IX.6.14). It is important to note that Augustine now has a different view of death as a believer from that which he had when his friend died when he was twenty-one and a Manichaean. Then he was inconsolable; now he can say with confidence that he has no fear or anxiety regarding his son's death because he knows that there is hope beyond the grave for the Christian.

Although Augustine does not go into detail regarding his baptism, he does tell us how he felt after the administration of this wonderful sacrament:

> And so we were baptized, and all our dread about our earlier lives dropped away from us. During the days that followed I could not get enough of the wonderful sweetness that filled me as I meditated upon your deep design for the salvation of the human race. How copiously I wept at your hymns and canticles, how intensely was I moved by the lovely harmonies of your singing Church! Those voices flooded my ears, and the truth was distilled into my heart until it overflowed in loving devotion; my tears ran down, and I was the better for them.[5]

In addition to the outstanding preaching of Bishop Ambrose, the church in Milan had gifted singers that produced wonderful music. Augustine is careful to note that he was "intensely moved by the lovely harmonies" sung at the church in Milan. This singing gift, however, would also become useful when the church in Milan was met with an unacceptable request by Emperor Valentinian. Shortly after Augustine's baptism, the boy-emperor Valentinian (influenced by his mother Justina) requested that Ambrose

5. Ibid.

hand over one of the churches under his care to the Arians. Ambrose and the Christians in Milan rejected this request, bringing about a standoff between the emperor and the bishop. Consequently, Ambrose was ordered to hand over the church immediately and to meet in person with the emperor regarding the latter's demand. Ambrose refused both of the emperor's requests, causing the emperor to send armed troops into the church to enforce his order. Augustine notes that in response to this standoff, Ambrose and his congregation stayed up all night singing hymns in order to prevent the take over of the church in question. Writing to Emperor Valentinian explaining why he did not come and speak to him in person, Ambrose informed the emperor that he was following the law laid down by Valentinian's father, namely, that matters regarding faith, or matters concerning a priest or a bishop, should be judged by other bishops (Ambrose, *Ep.* 21.2). Moreover, he informed the emperor that he could not give the church over to the Arians because they believed, as did the heathens, that Christ was a creature, making them heretics according to the Council of Nicaea (Ambrose, *Ep.* 21.13–14).[6] In another letter, written to his sister, Ambrose goes into more detail regarding the churches in question (Ambrose, *Ep.* 20), writing that initially the emperor demanded that the newly erected basilica within the wall of the church grounds be handed over. When Ambrose and his congregation refused, the prefect came and requested that they at least give up the smaller Portian basilica, which they also refused to hand over (Ambrose, *Ep.* 20.1–3). On the following Sunday, some of the members of the congregation took matters in their own hands and grabbed an Arian priest named Castulus, with the intent of harming him. When Ambrose became aware of this, he immediately sent deacons and priests to rescue the Arian priest, insisting that the people should not shed blood on behalf of the church but rather trust God for their deliverance (Ambrose, *Ep.* 20.5). After narrating several tense moments between the Christians of Milan and the imperial troops, Ambrose described their final deliverance:

> For whose gift is this, whose work is this but Yours, Lord Jesus? You saw armed men coming to your temple; on the one hand the People wailing and coming in throngs so as not to seem to surrender the Basilica of God, on the other hand the soldiers ordered to use violence. Death was before my eyes, lest madness should gain any footing while things were thus. You, O Lord, came between,

6. For a thorough discussion of Arius and Arianism, see Hanson, *Christian Doctrine.*

and made of two one. You restrained the armed men, saying, if you run together to arms, if those shut up in my temple are troubled, "what profit is there in My blood?" Thanks then be unto You, O Christ. No ambassador, no messenger, but You, O Lord, have saved Your people, "You have put off my sackcloth and girded me with gladness."[7]

Augustine tells us that his mother Monnica was among those believers ready to die with their bishop rather than hand over a Christian church to persons they considered heretics (*Conf.* IX.7.15).

Augustine maintains that other events, directed by God, helped calm the aggression of the emperor's mother Justina. When Bishop Ambrose was asked to consecrate a new basilica, the people requested that he consecrate it as he had consecrated a church in Rome. To which he responded "Certainly I will if I find any relics of martyrs." Ambrose reports that then "a kind of prophetic ardor seemed to enter my heart."[8] Having been divinely led to the bodies of Gervasius and Protasius, he had them dug up and transferred to the basilica of Fausta. And while they were there overnight, several miracles were reported. Many people that were tormented by evil spirits were healed, and others with various infirmities were cured. Moreover, when the martyrs' bodies were moved the next day to another basilica, a blind man named Severus was reported to have gained his sight. When he heard that the holy relics were being transferred, he asked that he be taken to the church where they lay. When he arrived, he took his handkerchief and placed it on the funeral brier and then placed his handkerchief on his eyes. His sight was immediately restored (*Conf.* IX.7.16). When news of his healing was broadcast around town, the faithful in Milan celebrated enthusiastically, while the Arians expressed denial and ridicule. Bishop Ambrose was so moved by the miracles of the martyrs that he ordered that their relics be placed beneath the altar that he had earlier reserved for himself. In his words:

> Let these triumphant victims be brought to the place where Christ is the victim. But He upon the altar, Who suffered for all; they beneath the altar, who were redeemed by His Passion. I had destined this place for myself, for it is fitting that the priest should rest there where he has been wont to offer, but I yield the right hand portion to the sacred victims; that place was due to the martyrs.

7. Ambrose, *Ep.* 20.21, trans. Schaff, *NPNF.* 10:918.
8. Ambrose, *Ep.* 22.1, trans. Schaff, *NPNF,* 10:937.

> Let us, then, deposit the sacred relics, and lay them up in a wor-
> thy resting-place, and let us celebrate the whole day with faithful
> devotion.[9]

Augustine was in Milan to witness the standoff between the believers in Milan and the emperor, as well as the healings conferred by the newly discovered martyrs. He believed that God used these miracles to demonstrate his power to the emperor and his mother and that as a result they ceased persecuting the church in Milan. One can only imagine how Augustine grew in respect and admiration for Bishop Ambrose after witnessing these incidents. Certainly, he had an excellent example of how a dedicated bishop should act in the face of adversity.

In closing book IX, Augustine discusses in some detail the life and death of his mother, Monnica. Earlier in his *Confessions*, Augustine tells us that she was a loving and dedicated mother who constantly prayed for his salvation. As has been narrated in a previous chapter, he came to realize that in the years when he thought God was silent, God was in fact speaking to him through his mother, though he would not listen. He now wants to speak about her in hopes that future generations may know this wonderful servant of God. However, before he goes into detail regarding her wonderful gifts, he pauses to inform us of a sin that nearly ruined her. As a young lady, she was responsible for a young mistress, in whom she did her best to instill discipline and restraint. In fact, she was so strict, Augustine recalls, that she would not even allow her mistress a drink of water between meals. Yet, while trying to instill discipline and restraint in her mistress, she found herself lacking discipline and restraint, for when she was asked to draw from the wine container so that the adults could have a drink, she began taking small amounts of the wine to wet her lips. However, this small amount soon increased so that she was drinking larger and larger amounts of wine each time she was asked to draw from the container. But as a skillful surgeon, Augustine recalls, God "cut away that diseased tissue in a single sweep" (*Conf.* IX.8.18). One day, while she was arguing with her young mistress, the latter called her "a wine-swiller." Those words cut her so deeply that, Augustine says, "my mother took heed to her disgraceful conduct and condemned it and threw it off at once" (*Conf.* IX.8.18). Augustine believes God was at work in this, using words that were meant to hurt to bring about a complete healing. Apart from this incident, Augustine has nothing but good things to say about his mother. Because her parents were Christian,

9. Ambrose, *Ep.* 22.13, trans. Schaff, *NPNF*, 10:940.

she was brought up in a Christian home. Yet, when she became of marriage-able age, she was entrusted to a husband who was not a Christian. Thus, she had the challenge of winning him over to Christ while showing patience as she put up with his many infidelities.[10] Because of her forbearance and dedication to God, she eventually won her husband, Patricius, to Christ. Concerning this, Augustine says, "She made it her business to win him for you by preaching you to him through her way of life, for by her conduct you made her beautiful in her husband's eyes as a person to be respected, loved and admired" (*Conf.* IX.9.19). Moreover, by her patience, she was able to deal with Patricius' hot temper. When Patricius got upset with something she said, she would patiently wait for him to calm down and then make her point, with much success. As a result, her quick-tempered husband never beat her, as husbands beat many of the other women in their town. When the other wives inquired as to why she was never beaten by Patricius, she counseled them on the actions she took, advising them not to speak to their husbands when the latter were upset but patiently to wait for them to calm down and only then to speak their mind. Augustine reports that the women who took her advice were no longer beaten by their husbands, while those who did not continued to be bullied and battered. In addition to teaching the women in her community how to exhibit patience, Monnica was also a peacemaker among them. Often when women were at variance with each other, she would listen to both sides and then try to bring them to a point of reconciliation. Because she was not a gossiper, the women could trust her in this role, and so she was often successful at bringing about peace.

From Augustine's account in his *Confessions*, it appears that his mother lived with him most of the time after his father's death. As a result, they were naturally very close to and supportive of each other. When they were together, Augustine tells us, she ran the household, probably helping raise her grandson and treating his friends as if they were all her children. No wonder that he called his mother a "servant of servants." Moreover, he insists that "everyone who knew her found ample reason to praise, honor and love her as they sensed God's presence in her heart, attested by the fruits of her holy way of life" (*Conf.* IX.9.22). Augustine certainly shared his mother with his friends that lived with him, and, as far as we know, it was a peaceful home, full of intelligent young men. One special moment stands out, however, when he and Monnica were alone together discussing his

---

10. Augustine's awareness of his father's infidelities is probably one reason why he does not speak glowingly of him.

newfound faith. In Ostia, preparing to return to Africa, they were looking out a window onto the garden below as they began discussing what the blessings of heaven might be like:

> Our colloquy led us to the point where the pleasures of the body's senses, however intense and in however brilliant a material light enjoyed, seemed unworthy not merely of comparison but even of remembrance beside the joy of that life, and we lifted ourselves in longing yet more ardent toward *That Which Is*, and step by step traversed all bodily creatures and heaven itself, whence sun and moon and stars shed their light upon the earth. Higher still we mounted by inward thought and wondering discourse on your works, and we arrived at the summit of our own minds; and this too we transcended, to touch that land of never-failing plenty where you pasture Israel for ever with food of truth. Life there is the Wisdom through whom all these things are made, and all others that have been or ever will be; but Wisdom herself is not made: she is as she always had been and will be for ever. Rather should we say that in her there is not "has been" or "will be," but only being, for she is eternal, but past and future do not belong to eternity. And as we talked and panted for it, we just touched the edge of it by the utmost leap of our hearts; then, sighing and unsatisfied, we left the first-fruits of our spirits captive there, and returned to the noise of articulate speech where a word has beginning and end.[11]

At the end of this wonderful experience, Monnica tells her son that heaven is the only place she desires now:

> For my part, my son, I find pleasure no longer in anything this life holds. What I am doing here still, or why I tarry, I do not know, for all worldly hope has withered away from me. One thing only there was for which I desired to linger awhile in this life: to see you a Catholic Christian before I died. And this my God has granted to me more lavishly than I could have hoped, letting me see you even spurning earthly happiness to be his servant. What now keeps me here?[12]

With those prophetic words, Monnica soon received what she earnestly desired. A few days later, she fell ill with a disease from which she was not to recover. Ultimately, she fell into a coma, but while awake for a few minutes she told her sons (Augustine and his brother) that they would

11. *Confessions*, IX.10.24.

12. Ibid., IX.10.26.

bury her in Ostia. Augustine's brother was displeased by this comment and insisted that their mother be buried in her own country. She thought this was silly and told both of them, "Lay this body down anywhere, and take no trouble over it. One thing only do I ask of you, that you remember me at the altar of the Lord wherever you may be" (*Conf.* IX.11.27). After making these wishes clear to her sons, she passed away peacefully. At her passing, her grandson Adeodatus began to cry but was asked to stop by Augustine and the others, who believed that it was unfitting to mark the death of a faithful Christian women with tears of sadness like the pagans who have no hope in the afterlife. So they had Augustine's friend Evodius lead a psalm appropriate to the occasion, and he sang *I will sing to you of your mercy and justice, O Lord* (*Conf.* IX.12.31). Augustine, of course, did cry later, but not until after the funeral, when he could weep in the presence of God alone. In a final tribute to his mother, Augustine prays for his mother as she requested and then offers a fitting eulogy to this unselfish woman of God:

> On the day, when her release was at hand she gave no thought to costly burial or the embalming of her body with spices, nor did she pine for a special monument or concern herself about a grave in her native land; no, that was not her command to us. She desired only to be remembered at your altar, where she had served you with never a day's absence. From that altar, as she knew, the holy Victim is made available to us, he through whom the record of debt that stood against us was annulled.[13]

---

13. Ibid., IX.13.36.

DISCUSSION QUESTIONS FOR CHAPTER 9

1. Discuss Augustine's opening praise. How does it relate to Augustine's new relationship?

2. Why do you think the author of this book calls Augustine's question regarding his free will odd? Do you agree or disagree?

3. Why did Augustine want to resign from his teaching post? And why did he care about what people might think about his actions?

4. What happened that gave him the perfect excuse he needed to quit his teaching post? Was that a coincidence or an act of God?

5. Discuss the death of Verecundus and Nebridius and how their deaths affected Augustine. What did he do to cope with his grief?

6. Discuss Augustine and his love for the Psalms.

7. Discuss the incident regarding Augustine's toothache. Why do you think he included this incident in his *Confessions*?

8. Discuss the relationship between Augustine and his son, Adeodatus.

9. Why does he not grieve over his son's death as he did over a friend's death when he was twenty-one and a Manichaean?

10. Discuss what Augustine did and how he felt after his baptism. Can you relate to any of this?

11. Why were Bishop Ambrose and the Christians in Milan dead set against giving up a basilica to the Arians?

12. What was the gist of Ambrose's argument to Emperor Valentinian for this refusal?

13. How did Ambrose finally get the victory in this situation?

14. What role did the martyrs Gervasius and Protasius play in this stand-off, according to Augustine?

15. Discuss the life and character of Augustine's mother Monnica.

10

Memory

Augustine begins book X with a declaration of his desire to know the God of Scripture and the maker of the universe more intimately:

> Let me know you, O you who know me; then shall I know even as I am known. You are the strength of my soul; make your way in and shape it to yourself that it may be yours to have and to hold, free from stain or wrinkle.[1]

Scripture says to the believer that Christ wants a church without spot or wrinkle (Eph 5:27). Perhaps Augustine has this Scripture in mind when he says, "Make your way in and shape it [my soul] to yourself." Now that Augustine is a member of the church, he is requesting that God assist him to become that special person that a Christian ought to be. He has accepted God's gift of holy continence and is now living as one who is married not to a wife but to the church. As a result, he desires that God shape him in the right way that he might be that mature Christian without spot or wrinkle. Certainly, this is his hope. In fact, from this hope, Augustine declares, "springs a joy that is well founded" (*Conf.* X.1.1).

In section 2.2 of book X, Augustine pauses to tell the reader what he hopes to achieve in his *Confessions*, why he believes the work is necessary, and what he hopes the reader will receive from it. First, Augustine tells us that his main desire and what he hopes to achieve in his *Confessions* is simply to speak the truth. This is important, for Augustine knows that God

---

1. *Confessions*, X.1.1.

loves the truth. Why? Because the person who seeks the truth will come to the light. If this happens, the *Confessions* are a benefit, for they will assist persons reading them to draw closer to God. But how will people know that Augustine is speaking the truth and so draw closer to God and receive this benefit, since he has many critics? Augustine anticipates this question, declaring, "I cannot prove that what I say is true, but all those whose ears are open to me by love will believe me" (*Conf.* X.3.3). Clark suggests that this statement was an attempt by Augustine to quiet his critics:

> Some of Augustine's first readers were prepared to accuse him of deliberate lies or at least of misrepresentation. The senior bishop of his region had expressed some (understandable) anxieties about his ordination as bishop after so little experience of the church, especially when nothing was known about his baptism in Milan and rather too much was remembered about his youth. His Do-natist enemies, as well as his former Manichaean friends, seized on this. A Manichaean, Secundinus, accused him of leaving the sect only from fear of persecution, not because their teaching had been refuted. A Donatist, Petilianus, said that Augustine was still a crypto-Manichaean and was further up the hierarchy than a simple "hearer."[2]

For Augustine, love is the bridge that he hopes will connect him with his readers, even though they might criticize him. And if they insist on judging him, Augustine says that this is all right too, as long as they do it with the fraternal love that he expects from a fellow Christian. For when fellow believers judge him, they will love in him the things that are pleasing to God, and pray for him in the areas of his life that need improvement. This is not so with the stranger or trouble maker. Augustine thus indicates that readers bear some responsibility in exchange for the benefit they receive from reading his *Confessions*. They must read his words in love and with the concern of a fellow Christian. Augustine also tells his readers that his *Confessions* are not just words that he chooses to speak. No, part of the process of confessing for Augustine is listening to what God is placing on his heart. So he declares, "I can say nothing right to other people unless you heard it from me first, nor can you even hear anything of the kind from me which you have not first told me" (*Conf.* X.2.2). This truth leads Augustine to ask, "Is hearing the truth about oneself from God the same as knowing oneself? And can anyone have this self-knowledge and still protest, 'It is not

2. Clark, *Augustine*, 53.

true' unless he himself is lying?"[3] Augustine seems to be saying that an intimate relationship with God will not only guide the confessor (himself in this case) as to what to speak but will also make the confessor aware of his or her true self.

In section 4.6 of book X, Augustine writes that many of his readers want to know not only about his past sins but also about the struggles he is dealing with now as he writes the *Confessions*.[4] As a result, the last benefit (or fruit) he hopes his readers receive stems from the fact that he is a fellow traveler on this journey with them:

> So then, when I confess not what I have been but what I am now, this is the fruit to be reaped from my confessions: I confess not only before you in secret exultation tinged with fear and secret sorrow infused with hope, but also in the ears of believing men and women, the companions of my joy and sharers in my mortality, my fellow citizens still on pilgrimage with me, those who have gone before and those who will follow, and all who bear me company in my life.[5]

After going into detail about what one can receive from the reading of his *Confessions*, Augustine turns to his love of God and his desire to know God more deeply. I suggest that this is no digression but rather an attempt to explore his current spiritual state more thoroughly. He begins this exploration by declaring: "I love you, Lord, with no doubtful mind but with absolute certainty. You pierced my heart with your word, and I fell in love with you" (*Conf.* X.6.8). This must have been an important confession for Augustine to make, for he had in his earlier life wandered far from the knowledge of God. He insists that he loves God with absolute certainty so that the reader may not misunderstand his next question: "But what am I loving when I love you?"[6] Before attempting a positive answer to this question, he tells us what he does *not* love when he is loving his God:

> Not beauty of body nor transient grace, not this fair light which is now so friendly to my eyes, not melodious song in all its lovely

---

3. *Confessions*, X.3.3. One could also conclude that since God is truth, that people will speak and follow truth to the extent they can hear and be led by God.

4. Augustine was 43 when he began writing his *Confessions* (397 CE).

5. *Confessions*, X.4.6.

6. Ibid., X.6.8.

harmonies, not the sweet fragrance draw me to carnal embrace: none of these do I love when I love my God.[7]

Yet after making this statement of what he does not love when he is loving his God, Augustine paradoxically counters his negative statement with an apparent denial of what he has just declared:

> And yet I do love a kind of light, a kind of voice, a certain fragrance, a food and an embrace, when I love my God; a light, a voice, fragrance, food and embrace from my inmost self, where something limited to no place shines into my mind, where something not snatched away by passing time sings for me, where something no breath blows away yields to me its scent, where there is savor undiminished by famished eating, and where I am clasped in a union from which no satiety can tear me away, this is what I love, when I love my God.[8]

The difference between the two statements above is slight, but very important. In the second statement, Augustine appears to be saying that he loves God as a kind of food, embrace, fragrance, etc., but he does so from his "inmost self." And this "inmost self" is his mind, where "place and time" are exposed to things that transcend time and place. This is key for Augustine, and he will go into depth in trying to understand the human mind and its ability to reach God. He begins his quest with creation and its connection to the God he loves:

> I put my question to the earth, and it replied, "I am not he";
> I questioned everything it held, and they confessed the same.
> I questioned the sea and the great deep,
> and the teeming live creatures that crawl,
> and they replied,
> "We are not God; seek higher."
> I questioned the gusty winds,
> and every breeze with all its flying creatures told me,
> "Anaximenes was wrong: I am not God."[9]
> To the sky I put my question, to sun, moon, stars
> but they denied me: "We are not the God you seek."
> And to all things which stood around the portals of my flesh I said,

7. Ibid.

8. Ibid.

9. Anaximenes of Miletus, one of the pre-Socratic philosophers, lived in the sixth century and died around 528 BCE. He taught that air is the source of all things. See Sacks, *Dictionary*, 21–22.

"Tell me of my God.
You are not he, but tell me something of him."
They lifted up their mighty voices and cried,
"He made us."[10]

After Augustine questions the earth and all its contents concerning God, he then turns his question inward and asks: Who are you in reference to me? And he answers by saying: "A man." See, here are the body and soul that make up myself, the one outward and the other within. Through which of these should I seek my God?" (*Conf.* X.6.9). Augustine realizes that it is with his mind (his inner self or inmost self) that he should seek God. For with his mind he can ask questions and seek understanding. Thus, Augustine declares, "human beings have the power to question, so that by understanding things he had made they may glimpse the unseen things of God, but by base love they subject themselves to these creatures, and once subject can no longer judge" (*Conf.* X.6.10).

Having declared that nothing made by God is to be confused with God, Augustine returns to his question.

> What it is then, that I love when I love my God? Who is he who towers above my soul? By this same soul I will mount to him. I will leave behind that faculty whereby I am united to a body and animate its frame. Not by that faculty do I find my God, for horse and mule would find him equally, since the same faculty gives life to their bodies too, yet they are beasts who lack intelligence.[11]

In the above statement, Augustine is saying that he must leave behind his physical nature to search for his God, since animals have a physical body but lack the intelligence to find God. He declares, "So then, I will leave behind that faculty of my nature, and mount by stages toward him who made me" (*Conf.* X.8.12). But what does Augustine mean when he says he will leave behind "that faculty of [his] nature and mount by stages" to God, to the one that made him? Augustine now understands that he must begin this search in the vast space of his memory or mind, which is his inner self. Thus his search for God, this quest for knowledge of and closeness to God, begins with an exploration of his inner self, his mind, and above all his memory: "Now I arrive in the field and vast mansions of memory, where

---

10. *Confessions*, X.6.9.
11. Ibid., X.7.11.

are treasured innumerable images brought in there from objects of every conceivable kind perceived by the senses" (*Conf.* X.8.12).

For the next several sections, Augustine discusses in much detail the greatness of our memory and how it can lead us to God. Augustine understands memory to be the storehouse of all kinds of impressions we receive, such as light, color, and various images. Now in regard to images, Augustine points out that when he sees an image (such as that of a mountain), the thing imaged does not itself enter our mind, but rather the image of the thing enters and can be recalled when we think about it. Moreover, Augustine argues that our memory has such immense space that it can hold all the things we learn in our academic life as well as those that enter the mind through our senses. When things enter our mind, they are "put away in wonderful compartments, and brought out again in a wonderful way when we recall them" (*Conf.* X.9.16). Yet there is another category of things (eternal truths perhaps) that exist in our memory, and concerning these Augustine admits that he does not know from what source or by what route they enter our memory (*Conf.* X.10.17). Regarding this phenomenon he offers the following explanation:

> We are therefore led to conclude that when we learn things which are not imbibed through the senses as images, but are known directly in their own reality inside the mind, as they are in themselves, and without the intervention of images, we are collecting by means of our thought those things which the memory already held, but in a scattered and disorderly way.[12]

One example of this phenomenon, according to Augustine, are the laws of mathematics. For mathematics is not impressed upon the mind by our senses; it has no color, sound, smell, etc. Yet the truth of mathematics is known within each person. Of course we hear the sound of the words when we speak about mathematics, but the truth concerning mathematics is different from these sounds (*Conf.* X.12.19). For these sounds concerning math could be heard in Greek or Latin or another language, and a person who speaks Greek but does not understand Latin will understand it in Greek but not in Latin. It is the "principle of number" that Augustine is speaking about here. For this principle transcends language, because it is a principle that allows an individual to think mathematically. In Augustine's view, this principle has a more real existence than things that can be

12. Ibid., X.11.18.

imaged, because it is an eternal truth that God has established in our mind. Augustine's thinking here shows the clear influence of Platonism.

Augustine now moves to a discussion of memory as it relates to our emotions. For example, people can remember how they were once in bodily pain, without being in pain when they recall the incident in their mind. Or people can remember being fearful and sad in the past, without being sad or fearful when they recall those incidents in the present. Pondering this, Augustine pauses to give a summary of what he has covered thus far:

> O my God, profound infinite complexity, what a great faculty memory is, how awesome a mystery! It is the mind, and this is nothing other than my very self. What am I, then, O my God? What is my nature? It is teeming life of every conceivable kind, and exceedingly vast. See, in the measureless plains and vaults and caves of my memory, immeasurably full of countless kinds of things which are there either through their images (as with material things), or by being themselves present (as in the knowledge acquired through a liberal education), or by registering themselves and making their mark in some indefinable way (as with emotional states which the memory retains even when the mind is not actually experiencing them, although whatever is in the memory must be in the mind too)—in this wide land I am made free of all of them, free to run and fly to and fro, to penetrate as deeply as I can, to collide with no boundary anywhere. So great is the faculty of memory, so great the power of life in a person whose life is tending toward death![13]

The second and third lines of the passage above are very telling, for Augustine again connects his memory and mind with his soul or "very self." He then goes on to describe the complexities of his self or mind. The mind, he says, has no boundaries, but can "fly to and fro"—we can assume he means "to and fro" in the spiritual realm seeking God.

Thus, it is from his mind or inner self that he makes the following assertion: "I will pass beyond this faculty of mine called memory, I will pass beyond it and continue resolutely toward you. O lovely Light. What are you saying to me? See, I am climbing through my mind to you who abide high above me" (*Conf.* X.17.26). Augustine is saying he will go *beyond* his mind to reach God, but he also realizes that in his search thus far he is in fact "flying to and fro" *in* his mind toward God.

13. Ibid., X.17.26.

This hints at a problem with his proposition as it has been stated thus far. For Augustine realizes that if he were to pass beyond his memory, he would forget God. And how shall he find God, once he is no longer mindful of God? For even if a person is told to remember something that they have forgotten, they can remember only it if it has not been forgotten entirely; when something is forgotten entirely, we will not remember it, even if we are reminded.[14] Thus, Augustine asks: How then am I to seek you—since going beyond my memory is unacceptable? Taking a somewhat different tack, he now asserts:

> When I seek you, my God, what I am seeking is a life of happiness. Let me seek you that my soul may live, for as my body draws its life from my soul, so does my soul draw its life from you. How then, am I to seek a life of happiness? It is not mine until I can say, "This is all I want; here is happiness."[15]

Augustine is now in a quest for the happy life, for it is here that he will find his God. But where can one look for this happy life, and is it somewhere in our memory? Augustine asserts that everyone, without exception, wants the happy life. This raises the question of where people come to know of this happiness, so that they can desire it—since obviously one cannot desire something if one does not know of its existence. Does the happy life exist in our memory? And if it does exist in our memory, Augustine asks, does this means that we were happy once upon a time? For example, were we all happy in Adam, before the fall?[16] And if this is so, did we lose our happiness after the fall? In any event, Augustine believes that the knowledge of happiness exists in our memory. But how? According to Augustine, we do not remember happiness in the way in which we remember Carthage, for the happy life is not seen with the eyes. The happy life is not perceived with our senses at all. Augustine contends that the happy life that he loves and desires is found in God only:

---

14. We have to be aware of how Augustine is using language here. When he speaks of something being forgotten, he is using the word "forgotten" in two ways. For Augustine, some things are not fully forgotten and so they can be remembered, when brought to our attention. However, when he speaks of forgetting something in the literal sense, then those things cannot be remembered, even if someone reminds us of them.

15. *Confessions*, X.20.19.

16. Augustine does not mention Adam by name but we know he is referring to Adam, for he says the following: "Were we all happy in the man who committed the first sin, in whom all died and from whom we are all born to misery?" (*Confessions*, X.20.29).

Far be it, Lord, far be it from the heart of your servant who confesses to you, far be it from me to think that enjoyment of any and every kind could make me happy. A joy there is that is not granted to the godless, but to those only who worship you without looking for reward, because you yourself are their joy. This is the happy life, and this alone: to rejoice in you, about you and because of you. This is the life of happiness, and it is not to be found anywhere else. Whoever thinks there can be some other is chasing a joy that is not the true one; yet such a person's will has not turned away from all notion of joy.[17]

Certainly Augustine is reflecting on his own life here, and how he had sought happiness in the wrong places. Earlier in his life, he had sought happiness in status, and later in the teaching of Manichaeism, and as a youth he had sought happiness in the fulfillment of his lustful desires. But now that he is a believer, he can say that he is experiencing true happiness because he loves God with absolute certainty. For what Augustine loves when he is loving his God is this: to rejoice in God, to rejoice about God and to rejoice because of God. This is the answer that he has been seeking. For the happy life cannot be found anywhere but in God alone. And it is in his mind, the place where Augustine has searched for truth and happiness all his life, that he has found God. Augustine also connects the happy life with the truth of salvation. For he says, "Now the happy life is joy in the truth; and that means joy in you, who are Truth, O God, who shed the light of salvation on my face, my God" (*Conf.* X.23.33). This is important, for the joy Augustine is speaking about is not an invisible or abstract joy found in the memory only; it stems from a relationship with God that began when he was saved. He acknowledges, however, that everyone will not come to the light or accept this truth, even though no one wants to be deceived and no one wants to be unhappy. He explains this predicament as follows:

They love truth when it enlightens them, but hate it when it accuses them. In this attitude of reluctance to be deceived and intent to deceive others they love truth when it reveals itself but hate it when it reveals them. Truth will therefore take its revenge: when people refuse to be shown up by it, truth will show them up willy-nilly and yet elude them.[18]

---

17. *Confessions*, X.22.32.
18. Ibid., X.23.34.

Augustine insists that this is the state of many people who do not come to the happy life; they will not allow the truth to reveal to them what they need.

In section 24.35 of book X, Augustine returns to his teaching on memory to offer the reader a summary of what he has discussed up to this point:

> How widely I have ranged through my memory seeking you, Lord, and I have not found you outside it; for I have discovered nothing about you that I did not remember from the time I learned to know you. From the time when I learned about you I have never forgotten you, because wherever I have found truth I have found my God who is absolute Truth, and once I had learned that I did not forget it. That is why you have dwelt in my memory ever since I learned to know you, and it is there that I find you when I remember and delight in you. These are my holy delights, and they are your gift to me, for in your mercy you look graciously upon my poverty.[19]

Augustine explains here that he came to know God the moment he was saved, but since that time he has sought a closer relationship with God through the meditative exercise of his mind. So it is in our memory that we meet God and it is there that we can deepen our relationship with God. Moreover, when we come to know God, we also know truth, because God is absolute Truth. These are God's gifts to us or, as Augustine says, our "holy delights." Augustine rejoices in knowing that God has honored his memory by making it his dwelling place. And even though God dwells in the mind, Augustine is quick to remind us that God is not the mind itself, but Lord and God of the mind.

After this thorough discussion, Augustine ends his consideration of memory with a fitting passage of praise that outlines his personal struggles with coming to the truth, with coming to know God:

> Late have I loved you, Beauty so ancient and so new,
> late have I loved you!
> Lo, you were within,
> but I outside, seeking there for you,
> and upon the shapely things you have made I rushed headlong,
> I, misshapen.
> You were with me, but I was not with you.
> They held me back far from you,

19. Ibid., X.24.35.

those things which would have no being
were they not in you.
You called, shouted, broke through my deafness;
you flared, blazed, banished my blindness;
you lavished your fragrance, I gasped, and now I pant for you;
I tasted you, and I hunger and thirst;
you touched me, and I burned for your peace.[20]

This is not only a paean of praise; it is also a poetic and dramatic account of how Augustine came to know God. It was late in his life (he was saved at 33), and he was looking in the wrong places (outward and not inward), but God broke through his deafness and saved him. And now he can say like David, *as a deer longs for flowing streams, so my soul longs for you* (Ps 42:1).

Earlier, in section 3.4 of chapter 10, Augustine informed us that his readers were interested in knowing what was going on in his life at the time of him writing his *Confessions*. Consequently, in the closing sections of the book, Augustine speaks of his current challenges. In addressing his life of continence, he says, "On your exceedingly great mercy rests all my hope. Give what you command and then command whatever you will. You order us to practice continence" (*Conf.* X.29.40). This statement upset Augustine's contemporary Pelagius because he thought Augustine was making excuses for not living a holy life. Augustine, however, says in the sentence that follows: "A certain writer tells us, *I knew that no one can be continent except by God's gift, and that it is already a mark of wisdom to recognize whose gift this is.*"[21] When Augustine was saved, God also saved him from his lustful behavior, so as to give him the gift of continence. But having this gift does not mean that he will automatically be successful in his fight against lust. There is an adversary ready to help him fall at any time. Moreover, Augustine also notes that his memory—that place where he meets God—is also a battle ground where sexual images, implanted from his previous lifestyle, attack him in his dreams. The gift does not eliminate the struggle, and so one can understand Augustine's desire for God to be merciful and to help him with what he knows God has both gifted and commanded him to do.

Next, Augustine addresses the challenges he has regarding his senses. For example, in regard to hearing, Augustine admits that he is often moved during worship more by the beauty of the melody than by the words that

20. Ibid., X.27.38.
21. Ibid., X.29.40.

are being sung, and he considers this not to be good. But he believes that for the most part he does not have a problem in this area. Likewise, he insists that the sense of sight, or, as he puts it, the concupiscence of the eyes, no longer poses a problem for him. Nor do the senses of smell or touch give him much trouble. But in the area of taste, Augustine admits he is constantly challenged. He finds the temptation of food more challenging to him now than sexual temptation. Sexual lust can be conquered simply by not participating in sexual behavior, but he must eat, and so he has to fight against gluttony at every meal. Concerning this challenge, Augustine offers the following both as a solution and as a way of understanding the issues involved:

> By fasting I wage a daily warfare, and habitually force my body to obey me, yet the painfulness of this is outweighed by pleasure, for hunger and thirst are pains of a sort, which like a fever burn and even kill unless we have recourse to the medicine of food; and since this is ready-to-hand through your comforting provision, whereby earth and water and sky are at the service of our weakness, what could be a calamity for us becomes instead an occasion of enjoyment.[22]

Augustine is aware that food is a blessing from God, but it is a blessing that he finds hard to control. To deal with this challenge, Augustine says he tries to treat food as if it were medicine; yet he admits that he fights daily against overeating. Thus, one of Augustine's greatest challenges at the time he writes his *Confessions* is the sin of gluttony.

Another challenge, which Augustine calls the third category of temptation, is the sin of pride. Yet before Augustine speaks of his weakness in this area, he mentions his progress under God's grace:

> Are we to regard this as a trivial fault? Can there be for us any route back to hope other than your mercy, of which we have proof already because you have begun to change us? You know how much you have changed me, for you began by healing me of the itch to justify myself, so that you could be compassionate to all my other iniquities as well, heal all my ailments, rescue my life from decay, crown me in pity and mercy and overwhelmingly satisfy my desire with good things. You crushed my pride by inspiring

22. Ibid., X.31.43.

in me reverential fear, and you made my neck submissive to your yoke.[23]

Augustine admits that God has crushed his pride in many areas, but particularly in his need to justify himself before others. Nonetheless, even though he has made much progress in curbing his pride, at least two areas continue to challenge him. The first is his desire for admiration. Augustine realizes that this is not a sin in itself, but it becomes a problem when people make the admiration they receive the cause of their joy. If a person does this, then this is no true joy at all, but a "shameful ostentation" (*Conf.* X.36.59). Likewise, when a person receives praise for a gift God has given him or her, the praise is acceptable, unless the person derives more joy from being praised than for possessing the gift that earned the praise. When a person does this, Augustine says, he is accepting a praise which is a sham in the sight of God (*Conf.* X.36.59). In such cases, Augustine insists, "even the one who extols him is better off than the one so esteemed, for the former at least appreciates God's gift in a human being, whereas the other prizes what humans give him more than the gift of God" (*Conf.* X.36.59). Because we are often tempted by the use of the tongue through the praise of others, Augustine offers the following self-assessment:

> You are Truth, and in you I see that if I am touched by the high opinion others hold of me, it should be not for my sake but so that my neighbor may profit thereby. And whether this is the case, I do not know. In this respect I know myself less clearly than I know you. I beg you to reveal myself to me as well, O my God, so that I may confess the wounded condition I diagnose in myself to my brethren, who will pray for me.[24]

In the area of pride, Augustine confesses to his readers, he can never be completely certain that his motivations are pure. Consequently, the sincere believer must constantly seek God's counsel and mercy to avoid the sin of pride.

In section 40.65 of book X, Augustine offers a thorough summary of what he has discovered in his search for God through his memory and offers the following clarification. "It is still my constant delight to reflect like this; in such mediation I take refuge from the demands of necessary

23. Ibid., X.36.58.
24. Ibid., X.37.62.

business, insofar as I can free myself."[25] This statement is telling because, though Augustine was a hardworking bishop and pastor and a prolific writer, he values free time to meditate on the deep things of God. In fact, Augustine goes on to say, "From time to time you lead me into an inward experience quite unlike any other, a sweetness beyond understanding."[26] Surely, book X is the fruit of those inward meditative experiences of sweetness that Augustine chose to share with his readers.

25. Ibid., X.40.65.
26. Ibid.

DISCUSSION QUESTIONS FOR CHAPTER 10

1. Discuss the following statement by Augustine: "Let me know you, O you who know me; then shall I know even as I am known."

2. What does Augustine say that he hopes to accomplish in the writing of his *Confessions*? And what does he hope the reader will receive from them?

3. Why did Augustine say it was necessary for him to listen to God before he confesses anything?

4. Why do you think Augustine made a point to say that he loves God with absolute certainty?

5. Discuss the two statements Augustine makes about what he loves and does not love when he is loving his God.

6. What are the two parts that Augustine says make up a person? Why is this important?

7. Discuss how images are brought into our memory.

8. What does Augustine say about things that enter our mind but are not images, as for example our knowledge of mathematics?

9. What is the happy life for Augustine? And why does he say every person without exception seeks the happy life?

10. Why does Augustine ask, "Were we all happy in the first man who sinned?" What is he getting at here?

11. What does Augustine finally say the happy life is?

12. Why does Augustine say, "Late have I loved you, Beauty so ancient and so new"?

13. Discuss Augustine's problem with food.

14. Discuss Augustine's progress and problems with pride.

15. Discuss Augustine's overall meditative approach to seeking God in book X.

11

Time and Eternity

BEFORE GOING INTO A through discussion of time and eternity in book XI, Augustine begins by confessing to God and to his readers his motivation for delving into such a topic:

> Why then am I relating all this to you as such length? Certainly not in order to inform you. I do it to arouse my own loving devotion toward you, and that of my readers, so that together we may declare, *Great is the Lord, and exceedingly worthy of praise.*[1]

Augustine also admits the limitations on his time and on his ability to understand such a challenging subject. Much of Augustine's time as a bishop had to be spent counseling his parishioners, preparing sermons, writing letters, and fulfilling other church duties, so his time for exploring topics of intellectual interest was undoubtedly limited. Nonetheless, his devotion to God and his desire to learn, causes him to press forward. But, before he does, he prays that God enlighten him as he seeks understanding:

> O Lord my God, hear my prayer,
> may your mercy hearken to my longing,
> a longing on fire not for myself alone
> but to serve the brethren I dearly love;
> you see my heart and know this is true.
> Let me offer in sacrifice to you the service of my heart and tongue,
> but grant me first what I can offer you;
> for I am needy and poor,

1. *Confessions*, XI.1.1.

114

but you are rich unto all who call upon you,
and you care for us though no care troubles you.
Circumcise all that is within me from presumption
and my lips without from falsehood.
Let your scriptures be my chaste delight,
let me not be deceived in them
nor through them deceive others.
Hearken, O Lord, have mercy, my Lord and God,
O Light of the blind, Strength of the weak—
who yet are Light to those who see and Strength to the strong—
hearken to my soul,
hear me as I cry from the depths,
for unless your ears be present in our deepest places
where shall we go and whither cry?
Yours is the day, yours the night,
a sign from you sends minutes speeding by;
spare in their fleeting course a space for us
to ponder the hidden wonders of your law:
shut it not against us as we knock.
Not in vain have you willed so many pages to be written,
pages deep in shadow, obscure in their secrets;
Not in vain do harts and hinds seek shelter in those woods
to hide and venture forth,
roam and browse, lie down and ruminate.
Perfect me too, Lord, and reveal those woods to me.
Lo, your voice is joy to me
your voice that rings out above a flood of joys.
Give me what I love;
for I love indeed, and this love you have given me.
Forsake not your gifts, disdain not your parched grass.
Let me confess to you all I have found in your books,
let me hear the voice of praise,
and drink from you,
and contemplate the wonders of your law
from the beginning when you made heaven and earth
to that everlasting reign when we shall be with you in your holy
city.[2]

At the conclusion of his prayer, Augustine poses a question to start the discussion: How did God make heaven and earth? Before Augustine gives his answer to this question, he admits that he wished he had Moses present to question him about the contents of the first chapter of Genesis. But since

2. Ibid., XI.2.3.

this is not possible, Augustine begins by asserting what he knows from his observation of things around him. He insists that because things in creation undergo change and variation, they must have been created. "For change and variation imply that something is made that was not previously there" (*Conf.* XI.4.6). Everything, therefore, that undergoes change was created by God and did not come into existence of its own accord.

Augustine continues his discussion of creation by asking what tools God used to complete creation. This question allows Augustine to make his next point: that God did not make heaven and earth as a craftsman makes things from earthly material, such as wood and clay; nor did God use heaven and earth or water or air to make heaven and earth, because they had not been created yet. Augustine points out that the craftsman who constructs various objects does not in fact create them; rather the craftsman simply stamps a form on matter already in existence and in possession of its being (*Conf.* XI.5.7). Thus, the creative act of bringing something into existence out of nothing belongs to God alone. Consequently, God's creative act is quite different from what humans do in working with material already in existence. Augustine insists that God is the creator of both the craftsman and the material he uses. Even the senses of perception that the craftsman uses to plan and carry out his work are the creation of God.

But if God did not create heaven and earth the way a human craftsman creates an object, how *did* God create heaven and earth? Augustine begins his response by declaring, "Clearly, then, you spoke and things were made. By your word you made them" (*Conf.* XI.5.7). That raises the follow-up question that Augustine anticipates from his readers: How did God speak in creating heaven and earth? And to this Augustine offers the following answer:

> Surely not in the same way as you did when a voice came from the Cloud, saying, *This is my beloved Son?* That utterance came and went; it had a beginning and an end. Its syllables made themselves heard and then faded away, the second following the first, and the third following the second, and so on in due order until the last one followed the others, and silence fell after the last.[3]

Augustine here contrasts God's act of speech at the baptism of Jesus (Matt 3:17) with the speech act by which heaven and earth were created. In the former case, words were spoken in time and in succession As a result, they had a beginning and an ending. The eternal Word, however, which

---

3. Ibid., XI.6.8.

spoke in creation has no beginning or ending. Thus, Augustine is making a distinction between words which are spoken in time and the eternal Word, which is Christ. Now regarding this eternal Word and creation, Augustine has this to say:

> You are evidently inviting us to understand that the word in question is that Word who is God, God with you who are God;[4] he is uttered eternally, and through him are eternally uttered all things. This does not mean that one thing was said, and then another thing, so that everything could be mentioned in succession; no, all things are uttered simultaneously in one eternal speaking. Were this not so, time and change would come into it, and there would be neither true eternity nor true immortality. I know this, my God, and I give you thanks for it.[5]

Augustine is certain that one difference between the eternal Word and common words we speak is that the eternal Word spoke in such a way that all things that needed to be created were done so by "one eternal speaking." This is important, because, as Augustine will argue again and again, there was no time before creation; therefore, the eternal Word could not be said to have spoken words that were subject to time. Arguing this point further, Augustine asserts:

> Lord, we know it, because insofar as a thing is no longer what it once was, or is not what it once was not, that thing is dying or rising to new life; but in your Word there is no cessation or succession, for all is truly immortal and eternal. Thus in that Word who is coeternal with yourself you speak all that you speak simultaneously and eternally, and whatever you say shall be comes into being. Your creative act is in no way different from your speaking. Yet things which you create by speaking do not all come to be simultaneously, nor are they eternal.[6]

Augustine continues his discussion by asking why things subject to change arise from the eternal Word, which is not subject to change. He admits that he does not know a full answer to this, but he does offer a partial explanation: "Everything which begins to exist and then ceases to exist does

---

4. Certainly, Augustine is referring to the prologue in John's Gospel (1:1–3) here: "In the beginning was the Word and the Word was with God, and the Word was God. He was with God in the beginning. Through him all things were made; without him nothing was made that has been made."

5. *Confessions*, XI.7.9.

6. Ibid.

so at the due time for its beginning and cessation decreed in that eternal Reason where nothing begins or comes to an end. This eternal Reason is your Word, who is 'the Beginning' in that he also speaks to us."[7] In other words, things subject to change are created through the eternal Word that does not change simply because God wills it so.

After Augustine explains how God made heaven and earth through the eternal Word, he proceeds to address a question posed to him as he was writing his *Confessions*: "What was God doing before he made heaven and earth"?[8] Now this question was an attempt by some (perhaps the Manichaeans) to deny the eternal nature of God. For they would argue that, if God was doing nothing before he created heaven and earth, why did God not continue in this state forever? They reasoned that if God decided to do something that he had not previously thought to do, then this would prove that the God of Scripture is not eternal (*Conf.* XI.10.12). Augustine responds to his adversaries that God's will is not a created thing but belongs to the very substance of God. Moreover, Augustine accuses his critics of confusing human time with God's eternity:

> People who take that line do not yet understand you, O wisdom of God and Light of our minds. They do not yet understand how things which receive their being through you and in you come into existence; they strive to be wise about eternal realities, but their heart flutters about between the changes of past and future found in created things, and an empty heart it remains. Who is to take hold of it and peg it down, that it may stand still for a little while and capture, if only briefly, the splendor of that eternity which stands for ever, and compare it with the fugitive moments that never stand still, and find it incomparable, and come to see that a long time is not long except in virtue of a great number of passing moments which cannot all run their course at once? They would see that in eternity nothing passes, for the whole is present, whereas time cannot be present all at once.[9]

The last line is telling: "in eternity nothing passes, for the whole is present." In other words, there is no passing of time in eternity. And if there is no passing of time in eternity, then it is silly to ask what God was doing before he created heaven and earth. Augustine clarifies this point further:

7. Ibid., XI.8.10.
8. Ibid., XI.10.12.
9. Ibid., XI.11.13.

> If we take "heaven and earth" to cover all that is created, I boldly make this assertion: Before God made heaven and earth, he was not doing anything; for if he was doing or making something, what else would he be doing but creating? And no creature was made before any creature was made. I wish I could know everything that I desire to know to my own profit with the same certainty with which I know that.[10]

Augustine here insists that one cannot speak of God doing anything "then" in reference to something done before creation, because "there was no such thing as 'then' when there was no time" (*Conf.* XI.13.15). Augustine also connects this eternity of God with the Son:

> Your years are a single day, and this day of yours is not a daily recurrence, but a simple "Today," because your Today does not give way to tomorrow, nor follow yesterday. Your Today is eternity, and therefore your Son, to whom you said, *Today have I begotten you*, is coeternal with you.[11]

Having clarified the difference between human time and God's eternity, Augustine turns to a thorough discussion of human time. He starts by asserting. "If nothing passed away there would be no past time; if there was nothing still on its way there would be no future time; and if nothing existed, there would be no present time" (*Conf.* XI.14.17). Thus, we have the past, future, and present time that everyone speaks about and knows very well. Now, however, Augustine goes deeper in his analysis of time by challenging his readers to consider in what way time really exists:

> Now what about those two times, past and future: in what sense do they have real being, if the past no longer exists and the future does not exist yet? As for present time, if that were always present and never slipped away into past, it would not be time at all; it would be eternity. If, therefore, the present's only claim to be called "time" is that it is slipping away into the past, how can we assert that this thing *is*, when its only title to being is that it will soon cease to be? In other words, we cannot really say that time exists, except because it tends to non-being.[12]

Augustine asserts here that "present time" is all we really have, and it is fleeting into the past at lightning speed. Following this line of reasoning,

10. Ibid., XI.12.14.
11. Ibid., XI.13.16.
12. Ibid., XI.14.17.

Augustine asks his readers how we can say that a hundred years is a long time in the future or ten days a short time in the past, when the future and the past do not exist: "On what grounds can something that does not exist be called long or short?" (*Conf.* XI.15.18). Augustine insists it is more accurate to say of a long duration of time in the future, "That will be long," and to say of a long duration in the past, "That was long." To further clarify his point, Augustine asks another question:

> Answer my questions, then. Is the present century a long period of time? Before you say yes, reflect whether a hundred years can be present. If the first of them is running its course, that year is present, but ninety-nine others are future and therefore as yet have no being. If the second year is running its course, one year is already past, another is present, and the remainder are still to come. In the same fashion we may represent any one of the intervening years of the century as present, and always the years that preceded it will be past, and those that follow it future, Evidently, then, a hundred years cannot be present.[13]

Augustine continues along these lines; making the same argument about a year, a month, and finally a day, until he concludes with the following:

> Even a single hour runs its course through fleeing minutes: whatever portion of it has flown is now past, and what remains is future. If we can conceive of a moment in time which cannot be further divided into even the tiniest of minute particles, that alone can be rightly termed the present; yet even this flies by from the future into the past with such haste that it seems to last no time at all. Even if it has some duration, that too is divisible into past and future; hence the present is reduced to vanishing-point.[14]

In the next section of book XI, Augustine continues his discussion of time by analyzing its relationship to the human mind. Although the past does not exit, because it has passed away, Augustine allows for the recovery of past events in our memory, which exists in the present:

> Nonetheless when a true account is given of past events, which is brought from the memory, it is not the events themselves, which have passed away, but words formed from images of those events

13. Ibid., XI.15.19.
14. Ibid., XI.15.20.

which as they happened and went their way left some kind of traces in the mind through the medium of the senses.[15]

Thus, we can remember our childhood or some other past event, and our thoughts about these events may be present, even though the events are now past and no longer exist. Now Augustine asks if in regard to future events there can be an occurrence in the mind similar to that regarding past events. Specifically, can a person (a seer or fortune-teller) speak of events in the future? Augustine will allow that we can have future events planned in our mind, but that until we carry them out they are nonexistent. He will also allow that certain events can be predicted based on signs and causes that already exist. For example, we can predict the rising of the sun at a certain time based on signs and knowledge we already have about the sun rising. Yet Augustine will not concede to any human the ability actually to speak of future events: "We must conclude, then, that future events have no being as yet, and if they have no being yet they do not exist, and if they do not exist it is absolutely impossible for anyone to see them" (*Conf.* XI.18.24).

Thus, from Augustine's perspective, fortune-tellers are dishonest when they claim to speak of future events. On the other hand, to see and to speak of future events is not impossible for God, because God is not subject to future or past time. In the Old Testament, God is indeed represented as speaking to his prophets concerning future events. And this was possible, because everything with God is present, an eternal "Today." Augustine insists that God is not hindered by time nor affected by the future, for God created time. God exists in the eternal present. Conversely, one can say that to be human is to be affected by time. Of course, the Christian hope is to experience eternal bliss with God, where time does not pass.[16]

Augustine thus argues that it is better to describe present time as the present of present things, to describe past time as the present of past things, and to describe future time as the present of future things (*Conf.* XI.20.26). Augustine connects this understanding with the human mind by asserting that the present of past things is memory, the present of present things is attention, and the present of future things is expectation. Augustine does allow and does not disapprove of people using the common language for speaking about time (past, present, future) as long as they know the true meaning behind those expressions.

15. Ibid., XI.18.23.

16. For further reading on Augustine's understanding of time and how it resolves the paradox outlined by Aristotle, see Sorabji, "Time."

In section 21.29 of book XI, Augustine declares that he wants to go still deeper and know the essence of time; he wants to know what "time itself" is. He first attempts to get at the essence of time by comparing it with the rotation of the sun and the moon, but is sorely disappointed. For he realizes that the movements of these objects are not itself time, but rather are movements within time. In proof of this, he adduces the account of Joshua praying that the sun would remain still until he could win a battle, pointing out that the sun may have stood still, but time kept on going. So his search for the essence of time continues. But before he goes on, he makes this confession:

> I confess to you, Lord, that even today I am still ignorant of what time is; but I praise you, Lord, for the fact that I know I am making this avowal within time, and for my realization that within time I am talking about time at such length, and that I know this "length" itself is long only because time has been passing all the while. But how can I know that, when I do not know what time is? Or perhaps I simply do not know how to articulate what I know? Woe is me, for I do not even know what I do not know![17]

Augustine next asks how it is possible to measure time. He first attempts to measure duration by comparing the time taken to recite a long poem with many stanzas to the time taken to recite a poem with few stanzas. Augustine discovers, however, a problem with this approach: a person with a drawl could actually take longer to read a shorter poem than a person who reads a longer poem quickly. Augustine then asserts that "time is nothing other than tension, but tension of what?" (*Conf.* XI.26.33). In some frustration, Augustine suggests that it is a tension of consciousness. This, however, does not resolve the fundamental problem with measuring time: that we cannot measure the future because it does not exist, we cannot measure the past because it no longer exists, and we cannot measure the present because it does not stand still (*Conf.* XI.27.34). This causes Augustine to return to the relationship of mind and memory to time and its measurement:

> In you, my mind, I measure time. Do not interrupt me by clamoring that time has objective existence, nor hinder yourself with the hurly-burly of your impressions. In you, I say, do I measure time. What I measure is the impression which passing phenomena leave in you, which abides after they have passed by; that is what I

17. *Confessions*, XI.25.32.

measure as a present reality, not the things that passed by so that the impression could be formed. The impression itself is what I measure when I measure intervals of time. Hence either time is this impression, or what I measure is not time.[18]

Augustine cannot say with certainly that he is measuring time with his mind; and he has his doubts, as expressed in his last line ("either time is this impression, or what I measure is not time"). Nonetheless, the closest he comes to understanding time is how it is held in the mind or our memory. So he reiterates some of what he has said earlier, but with clarification:

But how can a future which does not yet exist dwindle or be used up, and how can a past which no longer exists grow? Only because there are three realities in the mind which conducts this operation. The mind expects, and attends, and remembers, so that what it expects passes by way of what it attends to into what it remembers. No one, surely, would deny that the future is as yet non-existent? Yet an expectation of future events does exist in the mind. And would anyone deny that the past has ceased to be? Yet the memory of past events still lives on in the mind. And who would deny that the present has no duration, since it passes in an instant? Yet our attention does endure, and through our attention what is still to be makes its way into the state where it is no more. It is not, therefore, future time which is long, for it does not exist; a long future is simply an expectation of the future which represents it as long. Nor is the past a long period of time, because it does not exist at all; a long past is simply a memory of the past which represents it as long.[19]

Augustine is not able to tell us what the essence of time is, nor how we can measure time as it passes. But he does inform us that when we speak of time as being long, this is true only because our memory or mind represents it this way. Augustine has also suggested to us in this book that we cannot speak of time before the creation of heaven and earth, because time did not exist before creation. Therefore, it is silly to speak of what God was doing "then," in reference to an act prior to creation, for there was no "then" before God created time. For God, time does not pass, for with God everything is present or, as Augustine says, an eternal "Today." Regarding God's stability Augustine closes book XI with this declaration:

18. Ibid., XI.27.36.
19. Ibid., XI.28.37.

Nothing can happen to you in your unchangeable eternity, you who are truly the eternal creator of all minds. As you knew heaven and earth in the beginning, without the slightest modification in your knowledge, so too you made heaven and earth in the beginning without any distension in your activity. Let anyone who understands this praise you, and anyone who does not understand it praise you no less.[20]

20. Ibid., XI.31.41.

DISCUSSION QUESTIONS FOR CHAPTER 11

1. Discuss Augustine's opening prayer as noted in our text.

2. How, according to Augustine, did God *not* create heaven and earth?

3. According to Augustine, how did God create heaven and earth? What is the difference between making something and creating something?

4. What are Augustine's points about the words spoken at Jesus' baptism and the Word spoken during creation?

5. How does Augustine answer this question: What was God doing before he created heaven and earth? Why is this question important for him to answer?

6. What does Augustine say in regard to past, present, and future time?

7. What does Augustine says about how we can measure present time?

8. How does Augustine connect the measurement of time with our mind?

9. Why does Augustine say that a person cannot speak of future events?

10. According to Augustine, how is it possible for God to speak of future events?

11. Does Augustine ever discover the meaning or the essence of "time?"

12. Why does his experiment using a long and a short poem to measure time fail?

12

Creation of Heaven and Earth

AUGUSTINE OPENS BOOK XII by confessing that he wants to know how heaven and earth were created. He believes that God will grant him this knowledge because Scripture has told the believer, *Ask, and it will be given you, search, and you will find; knock, and the door will be opened for you* (Matt 7:7). Well, Augustine is both knocking and seeking knowledge about the very creation of the world in book XII.

In book XI, Augustine spoke at length about how God created heaven and earth through his Word. He informed us that the Word created the world not in successive pronouncements but in one eternal speaking. Now Augustine continues his quest for understanding the act of creation but turns his focus to a more speculative exegesis of Genesis chapter 1:1–2: *In the beginning God created the heaven and the earth. 2) And the earth was without form, and void; and darkness was upon the face of the deep. And the Spirit of God moved upon the face of the waters.* Augustine focuses particularly on v. 2 and how he might harmonize it with v. 1. For example, what does it mean to say that the earth was formless (without form) and void, when in v. 1 the creation of heaven and earth appears to be presented as a single and complete act? Augustine harmonizes these verses by suggesting that God used this formlessness as part of the creation process: "Before you imparted form and distinction to that formless matter there was nothing— no color, no shape, no body, no spirit" (*Conf.* XII.3.3). Yet he goes on to say that this formlessness was not nothing at all, for there was some kind of undifferentiated formlessness that had sufficient substance that God could use it:

> What could this be called? How could the meaning of that statement be conveyed to slower minds, except by some similar expression? Nowhere in the world can anything be found more akin to total formlessness than "earth" or the "deep." Lying so far below us they are less distinctive than other, radiant, lofty objects and all resplendent things. I am therefore justified, I think, in assuming that when the earth is said to be *invisible and unorganized*, this is a convenient way of making clear to people what formless matter is, the matter which [God] had created undifferentiated in order to make from it the world in all its form and distinction.[1]

The last line is very telling, since Augustine says that God used this formless matter to make from it the world in all its form and distinction. At first glance, one might wonder if Augustine is contradicting himself here, since he repeatedly insists in his *Confessions* that God created heaven and earth out of nothing. Augustine states, however, that this formless matter was God's creation, and so he continues to uphold God's creation of heaven and earth from nothing, though with an intermediate step of the creation of formless matter. He clarifies this point in section 8.8 of book XII, but he first focuses on explaining the concept of formlessness:

> I dubbed "formless" not something that really lacked all form, but that had a kind of form from which, if it were to appear, my gaze would turn away as from something weird and grotesque, and liable to upset weak human sensibility very badly. But what I thus imagined was not formless in the sense that it lacked all form, but formless only by comparison with other things of fairer form; and clear thinking was beginning to convince me that I must eliminate the last vestiges of form entirely if I wished to gain a notion of what true formlessness would be. And this I could not do. I would have found it easier to deem anything that entirely lacked form nonexistent, than to conceive of something midway between form and nothingness, neither formed existence nor nothingness, formless and all but non-existent.[2]

Augustine also informs his readers that God has given him other information on this subject, but he does not feel inclined to share it, since his

1. *Confessions*, XII.4.4.
2. Ibid., XII.6.6.

readers might not have the stamina to take it all in. He is probably correct in this assessment.

In section 7.7 of book XII, Augustine returns to his focus on God, admitting that even if he does not know exactly how formless matter was used in the creation process, he does know and will confess that all things are derived from God and were made out of nothing by God. Yet they were not created from the substance of God, for something created from the substance of God would be equal to God and to the Son. So heaven and earth were created out of nothing or out of this formless matter that is like a nothing. For apart from God, nothing existed from which God could make anything that he did not create:

> Apart from yourself nothing existed from which you might make them, O God, undivided Trinity and threefold Unity, and therefore you made heaven and earth out of nothing—heaven and earth, a great thing and a small thing, because you are omnipotent and your goodness led you to make all good things, a mighty heaven and a tiny earth.[3]

Now in section 8.8 of book XII, Augustine mentions, if only briefly, a place called "heaven's heaven." This heaven in not mentioned in Genesis 1:1–2, but one possible translation of Psalm 115:16 is "heaven's heaven belongs to the Lord"; this is the translation found in the Vulgate and so may have been the reading in the Latin Bible Augustine used. Augustine says that this place is for the Lord, perhaps a way of saying this is where God resides. He also insists that this heaven's heaven was created before time. Yet in returning to the heaven and earth of Genesis 1, Augustine attempts to harmonize his idea of formlessness in Genesis 1:2 with his conviction that God created the world out of nothing: "For you, Lord made the world from formless matter, and that formless matter that was almost nothing at all you made from nothing at all, intending to create from it all the great things which fill us humans with wonder" (*Conf.* XII.8.8).

This formless matter was created out of nothing, and from it God brought form to things that had no form. Either way, God started with nothing and by his omnipotence created what he desired. However, there is another point Augustine makes in regard to this formlessness: "Where there is no form, neither is there order, and nothing comes or passes away; and where this does not happen there are certainly no days, nor any variation between successive periods of time" (*Conf.* XII.9.9). In other words,

---

3. Ibid., XII.7.7.

before the creation of the world, when it was formless and void, there was no time. After this declaration, Augustine breaks forth into praise before he continues:

> O Truth, illumination of my heart,
> let not my own darkness speak to me!
> I slid away to material things, sank into shadow,
> yet even there, even from there, I loved you.
> Away I wandered, yet I remembered you.
> I heard your voice behind me, calling me back,
> yet scarcely heard it from the tumult of the unquiet.
> See now, I come back to you,
> fevered and panting for your fountain.
> Let no one bar my way,
> let me drink it and draw life from it.
> Let me not be my own life:
> evil was the life I lived of myself;
> I was death to me; but in you I begin to live again.
> Speak to me yourself, converse with me.
> I have believed your scriptures,
> but those words are full of hidden meaning.[4]

Again, the last line is telling, for Augustine believes that there is much information in the Scriptures that he has yet to grasp fully. Nonetheless, after making this declaration, he mentions at least three things of which he is fairly certain regarding his knowledge of God. For example, twice in section 11.11 and once in section 11.12 of book XII, Augustine makes the following declaration: "Loud and clear have you spoken to me already in my inward ear," and he goes on to mention what God has told him there. First, God is eternal, and therefore no change can affect God. In addition, God's will does not change with the times: "For a will that can be some-times one thing, sometimes another, is not immortal" (*Conf.* XII.11.11). But God's will is immortal. Second, even though God has made all natures and substances, they have a different substance from God, and therefore any change in created things does not affect God. For in our weakness, we are often quick to move away from God and sin. Yet while our disobedience can affect us, it does not in any way disturb the order of God's reign. Third, no creature is coeternal with God, not even those beings whose entire plea-sure is in God alone and who have the privilege of being in God's presence.[5]

---

4. Ibid., XII.10.10.

5. Here, Augustine is likely referring to the angelic beings that share heaven with

Concerning the privilege of these creatures, Augustine says, "Your house-hold has never journeyed to any far country, and though it is not coeternal with you, yet by holding fast to you increasingly and without wavering it suffers none of the vicissitudes of time; from this let any soul capable of grasping it learn how far above all temporal change are you, the eternal" (*Conf.* XII.11.13).

Augustine now recapitulates some of the points he has been making up to this point:

> From this formlessness were to be made another heaven[6] and the visible, organized earth, and the beauty of fully formed water, and whatever else would thereafter constitute our world. In the making of this world a succession of days is mentioned, because the nature of these things is such that temporal succession is needed in their case to bring about ordered modification of motion or form.[7]

Recall Augustine's insistence that before heaven and earth were created, when there were formlessness and void, there was no time. Yet as the earth is being created we hear of a succession of days and therefore of time. Augustine believes that the biblical text indicates this, pointing out that by "recording that on the second day a vault was established and called 'heaven' or 'sky,' it indicates of what heaven it had been speaking before it began to count the days" (*Conf.* XII.13.16).

In the next several sections, Augustine discusses some of the disagree-ments persons had lodged against him regarding his exegesis of Genesis 1:1–2 and some of the points on which they agree. For example, they agree with Augustine that God's will and substance are the same. They agree that God willed everything once only and all together and eternally, and not in repetitive fashion. And they agree on many other things as well, but there is one point in which Augustine records his rivals' opposition:

> "Although your assertions are true," they say, "it was not those two realities that Moses had in mind when in response to the reveal-ing Spirit he said, *In the beginning God made heaven and earth.* By the name *heaven* he did not mean to indicate the spiritual or intellectual creation which unceasingly contemplates the face of God, nor did he indicate formless matter by the name *earth.* . . . By *heaven and earth* he intended to signify this whole visible world

God.

6. He says another heaven, to distinguish it from heaven's heaven of Ps 115:16.

7. *Confessions*, XII.12.15.

in brief and comprehensive terms first of all," they say, "so that afterward, by means of a series of days, he could enumerate one by one all those things which it pleased the Holy Spirit to have mentioned separately in this way. The race to whom he was speaking was crude and of carnal disposition; they were the kind of people to whom he judged it impossible to convey an idea of any works of God other than visible ones."[8]

Augustine replies by asking his critics if it is all right to speak of the invisible and unorganized earth that is noted in Genesis 1:2 as formless matter. They agree that this is not an unreasonable interpretation. Augustine then proceeds to offer several interpretations of Genesis 1:1–2 that differ but that all contain a measure of truth. He then concludes by asking: "What harm is there if a reader holds an opinion which you [God], the light of all truthful minds, show to be true, even though it is not what was intended by the author, who himself meant something true, but not exactly that?" (*Conf.* XII.18.27).

We must not believe that Augustine believed all Scripture could be given several equally true interpretations. But in regard to the passage in question, Genesis 1:1–2, Augustine believes there are truths there that even Moses may not have intended. Having said that, Augustine then outlines in section 19.28 of book XII nine points that he believes are true regarding creation. They also act as a summary of his teaching:

> 1. "That God made heaven and earth, And it is true that your Wisdom,[9] in whom you made all things, is the Beginning."
>
> 2. "That this visible world consists of the great regions we call heaven and earth, and that these names, 'heaven' and 'earth,' can be used as a brief, compendious phrase to connote all the natural things made and created within them."
>
> 3. "That every changeable thing suggests to us the notion of a certain formlessness, whereby that creature can receive form, or can be changed and transformed into something else."
>
> 4. "That any being which holds fast to immutable[10] form with such constancy that, though changeable in itself, it does not change, is not subject to variations of time."

8. Ibid., XII.17.24.

9. Wisdom here probably refers to Christ, the Word.

10. Augustine is probably referring to the angelic beings that live in the presence of God.

5. "That formlessness, which is close to nothingness, cannot experience any passage of time either."

6. "That a substance from which something else is made can by a certain convention of speech be given proleptically the name of the thing which is to issue from it: hence the formless matter from which heaven and earth were made could have been called 'heaven and earth.'"

7. "That out of all formed creatures, nothing is nearer to formlessness than earth and the deep."

8. "That [God], from whom all things come, made not only what is created and formed, but also matter with the potential to be created and formed."

9. "That anything which is formed from what is unformed is formless first, and then formed."[11]

After Augustine has laid out what he believes are basic truths on how God created heaven and earth, he proceeds to offer various interpretation of Genesis 1:1–2. However, he will insist that some opinions are questionable if they do not follow a certain logic. For example, Augustine believes that whatever one's interpretation of the scriptural text, it must "distinguish between what precedes in virtue of eternity, what precedes in time, what has precedence in the order of choice, and what has a purely logical priority" (*Conf.* XII.29.40). Thus, in regard to eternity, there is an order in which God precedes all things. In regard to time, it is only natural that flowers appear before fruit. In the order of choice, the fruit takes precedence over the flower. Finally, in logical priority, sound precedes the song. Augustine uses the fourth example, regarding a song, to make several points about creation:

> When someone is singing we hear sound and song both at once; it is not as though formless noise were heard first and then given the form of the song. If some kind of sound is audible in advance, it dies away, and then there will be nothing of it left which you could take up again and compose into a song by employing your musical skill. The song, therefore, happens in its sound, and this sound is the matter of the song. This very sound is what is formed so as to become song. And therefore, as I was saying, the matter, sound, has priority over the form that is sung, but not a priority in the

---

11. *Confessions*, XII.19.28. All nine points are taken from this section. They serve as a good summary of Augustine's teaching on creation up to this point.

sense of having power to create, for the sound is not the composer
of what is to be sung; it is merely made available to the mind of the
singer by the bodily organ he uses when he sings. Neither has the
sound any temporal priority, for it is uttered simultaneously with
the song. Nor has it any precedence in the order of choice, for no
one would think sound more excellent than song, since the song is
not mere sound, but sound endowed with beautiful form. But the
sound does have logical priority because it is not the song that is
given form to make it into sound, but the sound which is formed
to turn it into song.[12]

Augustine provides this rather lengthy explanation to help readers
understand the creative process. For example, just as sound is used to make
a song, so was formless matter used to create form in heaven and earth.
And as sound has logical priority in the making of a song, so does formless
matter have priority to what is formed from it. But Augustine insists that
neither has priority in the sense of having power to create; for the sound is
not the composer, but rather the singer. Likewise, the formless matter did
not create anything on its own, but God, who created the formless matter,
also controlled (created) what was formed from it. Thus, primal matter was
made first (as the existence of sound preceded the song) and called "heaven
and earth" because from it heaven and earth were made. Yet Augustine will
not allow us to say that formless mater came first in regard to time because
when there was formlessness, there was no time. But once time began to
exist, we can observe within time both matter and form (*Conf.* XII.29.40).

After offering this extensive analysis of Genesis 1:1–2, citing both his
own understanding and the opinion of others, Augustine closes book XII
with a prayer for guidance for himself and his rivals:

But as for us, Lord, we beg you to point out to us either that sense
which he intended or any other true meaning which you choose,
so that whether you take occasion of these words to make plain to
us the same thing you showed him, or something different, you
still may feed us and no error dupe us.[13]

The last few words are telling, Augustine believes there are several ways
to interpret the creation narrative; nonetheless, what he desires most while
searching out the hidden meaning of Scripture is that he not be duped.

---

12. Ibid., XII.29.40.
13. Ibid., XII.13.43.

STUDY QUESTIONS FOR CHAPTER 12

1. How is Augustine's discussion about the creation of the world in book XII different from that of book XI?

2. Discuss Augustine's understanding of the formless matter in Genesis 1:2.

3. According to Augustine, what is the heaven's heaven?

4. What does Augustine say about time and formlessness?

5. What are the three things Augustine says he is fairly certain about?

6. Discuss the nine truths mentioned in section 19.28 of book XII.

7. Discuss Augustine's use of "sound and song" to help readers understand creation.

13

Hidden Meanings in God's Creative Act

AUGUSTINE BEGINS THE LAST book of his *Confessions* in the same manner as he began the first: by praising God for what he is continuing to learn and rejoicing over the many blessings he has mercifully received from his creator:

> Upon you I call, O God, my mercy, who made me and did not forget me when I forgot you. Into my soul I call you, for you prepare it to be your dwelling by the desire you inspire in it. Do not forsake me now when I call upon you, who before ever I called on you forestalled me by your persistent, urgent entreaties, multiplying and varying your appeals that I might hear you from afar, and turn back, and begin to call upon you who were calling me. You have blotted out all the evils in me that deserved your punishment, Lord, not requiting me for the work of my hands, by which I defected from you to my own unmaking, and you have anticipated all my good actions, rewarding the work of your own hands that made me; for before ever I was, you were; I did not even exist to receive your gift of being; yet lo! now I do exist, thanks to your goodness.[1]

Augustine's statement at the end of this passage that he owes his very existence to God's goodness is important, for it leads Augustine to ask after God's purpose in creating him: "Did you will me to serve you so that you might be spared fatigue in your work, or because your power might be

---

1. *Confessions*, XIII.1.1.

diminished if my homage were wanting to it?" (*Conf.* XIII.1.1). The answer, of course, is that God did not create men and women because of any need on God's part. On the contrary, God created men and women that they may serve and worship their creator, and in so doing enjoy well-being. In fact, all of God's creative acts were done solely out of God's goodness and mercy. Augustine insists (perhaps against the Manichaeans) that God did not have to create anything, nor did any creature have any "preemptive claim" to God. How could they, when they were not yet created? For anything that does not exist cannot make any claim on the eternal creator who exists always and forever (*Conf.* XIII.2.3).

Throughout book XIII, Augustine discusses God's creation and various hidden or allegorical meanings that he believes can be extracted from Scripture. For instance, one of the first things God is said to have created is light. Genesis 1:3 in the Latin Vulgate says, *Let there be light, and light was made.* Now regarding this creative act, Augustine says, "It seems to me reasonable to refer this to your spiritual creation, which was already alive in some fashion and capable of receiving your illumination" (*Conf.* XIII.3.4). Augustine does not say in what way this spiritual creation was alive, but he does say that it was indebted to God on at least two accounts: one, for receiving life from its creator; and two, for changing from an inferior to a better state by being converted to God (*Conf.* XIII.3.4). Augustine insists, however, that even though God's creatures can change (hopefully from worse to better), this is not so with God. For God is in no need of change, because God is perfect goodness and truth.

In section 5.6 of book XIII, Augustine uses his consideration of creation to understand the Trinity. In book XI, Augustine spoke of the Trinity with an emphasis on the Word, and in book XII with an emphasis on the Father. Now in book XIII he discusses the Trinity with an emphasis on the Holy Spirit:

> Ah, now I have found what I was looking for! In symbolic form a Trinity now dawns clear for me, the Trinity which is yourself, my God. You, Father, made heaven and earth in that Beginning who originates our wisdom, that is to say in the Wisdom who is your Son, coequal and coeternal with yourself. . . . I understood already that the name "God" signified the Father who made these things, and the name "Beginning"[2] the Son in whom he made them; and

2. Notice that Augustine has several names for the Son. He is called: the Word, Beginning, and Wisdom. The name "Beginning" is very creative here, for when the Scripture (Gen 1:1) says, "*In the Beginning God created*": we can easily understand this to mean: In

believing as I did that my God is a Trinity, I sought for a Trinity among his holy utterances. And there was your Spirit poised above the waters! Here, then, is the Trinity who is my God: Father, Son and Holy Spirit, creator of the whole created universe.[3]

Augustine has found the Trinity in creation that he was looking for, but he wonders why the Holy Spirit was mentioned last and described as hovering over the waters. So he asks:

I beg you through Charity, our mother, I beg you to tell me, why was it that only after naming heaven, and earth, and the invisible and unorganized earth, and the darkness over the deep, did your scripture mention your Spirit last of all? Was it because it had to be introduced in such a way that he could be described as poised overhead? This could not be said of him unless something else was mentioned first, over which your Spirit could hover.[4]

Augustine, dissatisfied with the explanation given in the last sentence quoted above, finds a tenable answer in the teaching of Paul:

Anyone with enough mental agility should here follow your apostle who tells us that *the love of God has been poured out into our hearts through the Holy Spirit who has been given us.* But then, minded to instruct us on spiritual matters, the apostle points out a way of loftiest excellence, the way of charity; and he kneels before you on our behalf, entreating you to grant us some understanding of the charity of Christ, which is exalted above all knowledge. This is why the Spirit, who is supereminent Love, was said to be poised above the waters at the beginning.[5]

In connecting the Holy Spirit hovering over the water in creation with the teaching of Paul in Romans 5:5, Augustine makes at least two important points: first, that it is the Holy Spirit that fills the believer's heart with love; and second, that this love of God, which is given us by the Spirit, is exalted above all human knowledge, as the Holy Spirit was exalted high above the waters at the beginning of creation. Moreover, the love we receive from the Holy Spirit enables the believer to walk in the love of God. But we must be careful, for there are two loves, one natural and one spiritual. The natural love leads us downward, and the love of the Spirit leads us upward. Thus, it

the Word (Beginning) God created the heaven and the earth.

3. *Confessions,* XIII.5.6.

4. Ibid., XIII.6.7.

5. Ibid., XIII.7.8.

is important to walk in the Spirit if we are to demonstrate the love of God. Because of this challenge, we would do well to consider Augustine's petition regarding this matter.

> Give me yourself, O my God, give yourself back to me. Lo, I love you, but if my love is too mean, let me love more passionately. I cannot gauge my love, nor know how far it fails, how much more love I need for my life to set its course straight into your arms, never swerving until hidden in the covert of your face. This alone I know, that without you all to me is misery, woe outside myself and woe within, and all wealth but penury, if it is not my God.[6]

Augustine shares a prayer that every sincere believer would do well to repeat often. For even though the love of God may be shed into our hearts by the Holy Spirit, it is still a daily challenge to walk in that love in a way that is pleasing to God. Before Augustine closes this section regarding the Holy Spirit hovering over the waters, he insists that the other members of the Trinity must have been present also over those waters, even though they were not specifically mentioned in Scripture as doing so. Yet Augustine will not allow in his interpretation that the Trinity hovered over those waters in any type of bodily form, nor will he allow that the Trinity hovered over a place. But again he asks: if it is true that the complete Trinity was there, why does Scripture mention only the Holy Spirit? Augustine answers his own question by saying; "Because, I think, in your Gift we find rest. . . . We are borne toward it by love, and it is your good Spirit who lifts up our sunken nature from the gates of death" (*Conf.* XIII.9.10). Perhaps Augustine is implying here that just as we speak of the peace of God and the rest of God as being in our hearts—which is not spoken of as a literal place—so the Holy Spirit is spoken of as hovering "as though he were in a place, when it is no place" (*Conf.* XIII.9.10). Augustine acknowledges here the limitations of language on this point.

In section 11.12 of book XIII, Augustine resumes his discussion of the Trinity, but now he challenges his readers to examine the trinity within themselves:

> I wish that they would turn their attention to the triad they have within themselves. It is, to be sure, a triad far distant from the Trinity, but I propose it as a topic on which they may exercise their minds, by way of experiment and in order to make clear to themselves how great the difference is. The triad I mean is being,

---

6. Ibid., XIII.8.9

knowledge and will. I am, and I know, and I will. Knowingly and willingly I exist; I know that I am and that I will; I will to be and to know. Let anyone with the wit to see it observe how in these three there is one inseparable life: there is one life, one mind and one essence. How inseparable they are in their distinctness! Yet distinction there is. Everyone has himself readily available for inspection; let each, then, scrutinize himself, and see what he can find, and tell me.[7]

Augustine challenges his readers to understand the trinity within themselves and to report back to him with their findings. Yet he cautions them again not to think that what they may find can in any way be compared with the true unchangeable Trinity. Nonetheless, he poses a series of questions designed to give his readers something to ponder in their search:

Do these three coexistent acts constitute the Trinity? Or are all three found in each Person, so that each is this triple reality? Or are both these propositions true, the simplicity and the complexity being reconciled in some way beyond our comprehension, since the Persons are defined by their mutual relationships yet infinite in themselves? Thus the Godhead exists and is known to itself and is its own all-sufficient joy without variation for ever, Being-Itself in the manifold greatness of its unity. Who can find any way to express this truth? Who dare make any assertion about it?[8]

In spite of his last line, saying one should not dare make any assertion about the Trinity, Augustine cannot help but make assertions himself. In fact he would spend over fifteen years writing a book devoted to this topic, *De Trinitate*.[9]

In the next section, 12.13, Augustine reminds us that it is in the names of the Trinity (Father, Son, Holy Spirit) that we administer baptism and are baptized: "For among us too has God in his Christ created a heaven and an earth: the spiritual and the carnal members of his church" (*Conf.* XIII.12.13). Augustine connects the creation narrative with the work of God in both the church and the life of the believer. For example, before the earth was formed, it was invisible and unorganized. For Augustine, this represents how humans were shrouded in darkness and ignorance. But just

---

7. Ibid., XII.11.12. For a more developed view of Augustine's ideas of the Trinity in mental images, see Augustine's *On the Trinity* (*De Trinitate*), books 9 and 10.

8. *Confessions*, XIII.11.12.

9. For an account of the length of time Augustine took to write *De Trinitate*, see Augustine, *Trinity*, 17–20.

as God said, *Let there be light* to the natural world, even so did God speak to our hearts bringing about a change in our lives. Augustine expresses it this way: "We were converted to you, and light dawned. See now, we who once were darkness are now light in the Lord" (*Conf.* XIII.12.13). Again, using the light metaphor, Augustine makes the following declaration:

> In the morning I will stand and see my God, who sheds the light of salvation on my face, who will breathe life even into our mortal bodies through the Spirit who dwells in us and has been mercifully hovering over the dark chaos of our inner being. By this we have received, even on our pilgrim way, the pledge that we are children of light already. Saved only in hope we may be, but we are home in the light and in the day. No longer are we children of the night or of darkness, as once we were. But you alone distinguish between us and the night-born in this present uncertainty where human knowledge falters, for you test our hearts, and call light "day" and darkness "night." Who but you can tell them apart? Yet what do we possess that we have not received from you, since from the same lump you have formed us for honorable service, and others for common use?[10]

In this passage, Augustine is comparing the change that takes place in every believer with the change that happened at the beginning of creation: as the Spirit hovered over darkness and chaos at the beginning of creation, even so has the Spirit who dwells in the believer been mercifully hovering over the dark chaos of our inner being. Of course, the Spirit did not allow us to stay in that condition of darkness and chaos. No, the Spirit made all of God's children who were "children of darkness" to become "children of light," just as the Spirit hovered over the dark waters of creation before God said, *Let there be light.* Augustine also uses this metaphor of light to speak of a believer's maturity in Christ. For Augustine, mature Christians can withstand full exposure to the sun—that is, devotion to the life of the mind—while the immature or sensual Christian can be content only to view the light of the moon and stars—that is, to deal solely with sensible matters (*Conf.* XIII.18.22).

In the following section, 18.23, Augustine offers yet another allegorical interpretation of the creation account, interpreting the Apostle Paul in light of Genesis 1:1. Here, Augustine appears to be comparing the day and night of creation with the mature and immature life of believers. He equates

---

10. *Confessions*, XIII.14.15.

the sun that rules the day with the gift of supernal wisdom enjoyed by the mature, while less mature Christians must be satisfied with the moon and the stars that represent the lesser but still necessary gifts enumerated in 1 Corinthians 12:9–10. On the distinction between mature and immature Christians, he alludes to Paul's words in 1 Corinthians 3:1, where Paul tells his fellow believers that he cannot speak to them in a spiritual way but only in a carnal way, for they are still baby Christians. Paul, who is more mature than they are, still speaks of himself as striving for improvement. In a sense, the more we grow in Christ, the more we come out of the abyss (*Conf.* XII.12.13–13.14)—again an allusion to the creation narrative. But we can only do this, Augustine insists, by allowing our minds to be renewed by God's Scriptures (Rom 12:1–2), thus allowing the spiritual to rule the carnal and the heavenly to cover the earthly. As believers, however, we have help on this journey, for the Holy Spirit has been sent from heaven through Christ, that God's gifts may cascade upon us (*Conf.* XIII.13.14). Here, Augustine is referring to the spiritual gifts that are noted in 1 Corinthians 12: 7–11. The Holy Spirit dispenses these gifts as he chooses, yet in comparison to creation, Augustine says, these gifts are like the stars of heaven. That is, as the stars shine in the heavens and give light to all, even so does the believer shine in the world when he or she uses the Spirit's gifts for the benefit of others. As Augustine compares the spiritual gifts of God to stars in the heavens, so he also compares the sky or vault of heaven to Scripture. For just as the sky is stretched out over the earth, even so is God's word "stretched above your people everywhere until the end of the world" (*Conf.* XIII.15.18). And this written word or Scripture will abide forever. Likewise, the Word (Son) will also abide forever, even though preachers will remain only for a little while and then perish. This is important, because Augustine wants his readers to know that we must rely on what is eternal, not on what is temporal. This truth rouses Augustine once again to give God praise:

> As you exist in all fullness, so too do you alone possess the fullness of knowledge: you unchangeably exist, unchangeably know and unchangeably will. Your essence knows and wills unchangeably; your knowledge is and wills unchangeably; your will is and knows unchangeably. It therefore does not seem fitting to you that the unchangeable Light should be known by the changeable being it illumines in the same way as it knows itself. This is why my soul is like an arid land before you, for it cannot illumine itself from its

own resources, neither can it slake its thirst from itself. So truly is
the fount of life with you, that only in your light will we see light.[11]

In his praise above, Augustine is careful to acknowledge his dependence on God. For without God, he admits, he is a dry and dark land (a desert) in need of the light and life that only God can give. Throughout his *Confessions*, and up to the last pages of this work, Augustine pleads for this illumination from his creator. We would do well to imitate him on this point.

In section 22.32, Augustine discusses the creation of humankind. His chief concern is to point out that humans were made not after the pattern of other humans but after the image of God. And because they bear that divine image, humans have the ability to make choices. As a result, they have the ability to do God's will or to be disobedient. However, if humans can follow Scripture, particularly Romans 12:1–2, then they can follow God. Yet this does not give even faithful Christians the right to judge others in regard to salvation, for only God knows who in the end will be saved and who will be lost. Nor is a believer to judge Scripture. According to Augustine, the Christian is to submit to Scripture and not to judge it, even the parts he or she does not understand. If we do not understand something in Scripture, Augustine has shown us many times throughout his *Confessions* what we can do: we can ask God for understanding. In fact, Augustine ends his *Confessions* with such a plea:

> What human can empower another human to understand these things? What angel can grant understanding to another angel? What angel to a human? Let us rather ask of you, seek in you, knock at your door. Only so will we receive, only so find, and only so will the door be opened to us. Amen.[12]

11. Ibid., XIII.16.19.
12. Ibid., XIII.38.53.

STUDY QUESTIONS FOR CHAPTER 13

1. Discuss how Augustine begins and ends his *Confessions*. Can we learn anything from this approach?

2. Why do you think it was necessary for Augustine to say God did not create men and women out of any necessity?

3. What does Augustine say about the Holy Spirit in book XIII?

4. How does Augustine connect the work of the Holy Spirit in our life down here with what the Holy Spirit was doing in creation?

5. Discuss Augustine's examination of the trinity that he found in each individual.

6. Discuss the questions he poses to his readers regarding the Trinity in the quotation cited.

7. Discuss some of Augustine's allegorical interpretations of natural light and Scripture.

8. What allegorical interpretation does Augustine offer regarding the gifts Christians receive from the Holy Spirit?

9. Why is it important for Augustine to say that humans were made in the image of God?

10. Discuss the last quotation the author cites from Augustine's *Confessions*. What can we learn from these words?

Bibliography

Ambrose. *Letters*. Translated by H. De Romestin et al. In *Nicene and Post-Nicene Fathers*, 2nd ser., vol. 10, edited by Philip Schaff and Henry Wace. Buffalo: Christian Literature, 1896.

———. *Sermon Against Auxentius on the Giving Up of the Basilicas*. Translated by H. De Romestin et al. In *Nicene and Post-Nicene Fathers*, 2nd ser., vol. 10, edited by Philip Schaff and Henry Wace. Buffalo: Christian Literature, 1898.

Athanasius. *The Life of Antony and the Letter to Marcellinus*. Translated and introduction by Robert C. Gregg. New York: Paulist, 1980.

Audi, Robert, ed. *The Cambridge Dictionary of Philosophy*. 2nd ed. Cambridge: Cambridge University Press, 1999.

Augustine. *Confessions*. Translated and introduction by Maria Boulding. Hyde Park, NY: New City, 1997.

———. *Confessions*. Translated, edited, and commentary by James J. O'Donnell. 3 vols. Oxford: Oxford University Press, 1992.

———. *The Trinity (De Trinitate)*. Introduction, translation, and notes by Edmund Hill. Hyde Park, NY: New City, 1991.

———. *Writings against the Pelagians*. Translated by Peter Homes and Robert Ernest Willis. In *Nicene and Post-Nicene Fathers*, vol. 5, edited by Philip Schaff. Edinburgh: T. & T. Clark, 1991.

BeDuhn, James David. *Augustine's Manichaean Dilemma*. Vol. 1, *Conversion and Apostasy, 373–388 C.E.* University of Pennsylvania Press, 2010.

Burris, Ronald. *Where Is the Church? Martyrdom, Persecution, and Baptism in North Africa from the Second to the Fifth Century*. Eugene, OR: Resource, 2012.

Clark, Gillian. *Augustine: The Confessions*. Cambridge: Cambridge University Press, 1993.

Hanson, R. P. C. *The Search for the Christian Doctrine of God: The Arian Controversy 318–381*. Edinburgh: T. & T. Clark, 1993.

MacDonald, Scott. "Petit Larceny, the Beginning of All Sin: Augustine's Theft of the Pears." Chapter 4 of *Augustine's Confessions: Critical Essays*, edited by William E. Mann. Lanham, MD: Rowan & Littlefield, 2006.

O'Connell, Robert J. *St. Augustine's Confessions: The Odyssey of Soul*. Fordham University Press, 1989.

O'Meara, John J. *The Young Augustine: The Growth of Augustine's Mind up to His Conversion*. 2nd ed. New York: Alba, 2001.

Plotinus. *Ennead 1V.–4.29: Problems Concerning the Soul*. Translated, introduction, and commentary by John M. Dillon and H. J. Blumenthal. Las Vegas: Parmenides, 2015.

Possidius. *Sancti Augustini Vita scripta a Possidio Episcopo*. Edited, introduction, and English version by Herbert T. Weiskotten. Princeton: Princeton University Press, 1919.

Sacks, David. *A Dictionary of the Ancient Greek World*. New York: Oxford University Press, 1995.

Sorabji, Richard. "Time, Mysticism, and Creation." In *Augustine's* Confessions: *Critical Essays*, edited by William E. Mann, 209–35. Lanham, MD: Rowan & Littlefield, 2006.

Tack, Theodore E. *As One Struggling Christian to Another: Augustine's Christian Ideal for Today*. Collegeville: Liturgical, 2001.

Wills, Gary. *Augustine's* Confessions: *A Biography*. Princeton: Princeton University Press, 2006.

———. "The Book of Memory." In *Augustine's* Confessions: *Critical Essays*, edited by William E. Mann, 195–208. Lanham, MD: Rowan & Littlefield, 2006.

Index